'At last Steve Bell has given us, i  s analysis of the track record of Chr l constructive and, if taken on board lead to a small revolution, repentan ...wai in Christian training for clergy and missionaries.'

Ron George, founder of People International,
World in Need, and the Eurasia Education Foundation

'Christian, Muslim, neither; does it matter? *Mountains Move* challenges us to re-examine what we think "we know" in the context of our history, hegemony, identity, personality, faith and practice. Adventurous, provocative and engaging.'

Katy Knight, Trustee, Mahabba Network, UK

'Steve Bell demonstrates an empathetic understanding of Muslim concerns, combined with a clear-eyed look at the difficult issues, and a willingness to be self-critical yet true to his faith.'

Richard McCullum PhD, Senior Fellow at the Centre for
Muslim-Christian Studies (CMCS), Oxford

'We are very much indebted to Steve Bell's night- and day-dreaming! In an original, easy-to-digest, experience-born style, this is a timely contribution. He even-handedly illustrates, analyses and comments in a way that is intellectually rigorous and gently persuasive. Muslims and others are, at heart, in pain. How can followers of Jesus best help?'

Rt Revd Dr Bill Musk, author and former bishop in North Africa

'We urgently needed this book, and Steve Bell is uniquely qualified to write it. Muslims see the signs of collapse in western culture and, as someone of African heritage, Steve spots the irony of the role assumed by white middle-class Christians who speak from a debased culture while thinking it is superior. I applaud Steve's unspoken frustration when they "speak" without the human friendship God uses to set the scene for the work only he can do.'

John Ray OBE, educator, analyst, social commentator and writer

'Finally, a book which sets the complexity of public discourse with Muslims in a social and historical context. I appreciate Steve's sensitive handling and wise counsel on the difference between American and British attitudes to polemics. This online growth area makes this book a must-read on both sides of the Atlantic for those who misunderstand it, are reticent to use it, or may be using it incorrectly.'

Jay Smith PhD, founder of Pfander, apologist, polemicist and trainer

'One million Muslims live around London where I live, but I know almost nothing about them. I'm so grateful for this book, which provides a map and a context to better understand my Muslim neighbours, myself and the world. But it's not just about understanding; it's also about opportunity, because there has never been a time when so many Muslims are open to Christ. This framework gives me confidence to reach out with the good news of the gospel.'

Rico Tice, Senior Minister – Evangelism,
All Souls' Church Langham Place

'The topography of Steve Bell's "mountains" is enlightening and humbling. There is a steep but rewarding learning curve here for those longing for a more honest and humble witness to Muslim friends.'

Revd Dr Chris Wright, Director of Langham Partnership,
scholar, author and speaker

Mountains Move

Achieving social cohesion in a multicultural society

Steve Bell

Paternoster:
thinking faith

First published 2021 by Paternoster
Paternoster is an imprint of Authentic Media Ltd
PO Box 6326, Bletchley, Milton Keynes MK1 9GG.
authenticmedia.co.uk

British Library Cataloguing in Publication Data

A catalogue record for this book is available from the British Library

ISBN 978-1-78893-218-9
978-1-78893-219-6 (e-book)

Cover design by Semnitz
Printed and bound by Bell & Bain Ltd, Glasgow

Scripture Sources

Other titles by Steve Bell include:

Grace for Muslims?
Gospel for Muslims
Between Naivety and Hostility (co-editor)

Prepare the way . . . make straight in the desert a
highway . . . Every mountain and hill [shall be] made
low; the rough ground shall become level, the rugged
places a plain.

Isa. 40:3–4

Contents

Foreword

The 'mountains' that Steve Bell identifies are major obstacles not only to meaningful and mutually respectful interaction between Christians and Muslims, but also to intelligent Christian engagement with western culture in a more general sense.

The topography of Steve's 'mountains' is enlightening and humbling, and his detailed historical and contemporary documentation and examples compel us to recognize the legacy of our past and some of the lunacy of our present.

There is a steep but rewarding learning curve here for those longing for a more honest and humble witness to Muslim friends, and for all who seek to 'listen' to our world while being faithful to God's word and the hope of God's grace.

Revd Dr Chris Wright
International Ministries Director, Langham Partnership,
scholar, author and speaker

Before We Start

This is a journalistic (and hopefully objective) scoping of our contemporary situation. The aim is to be balanced, fair and accessible to *all* who are fair-minded, whether they are people of faith or not. There is some straight talking to secularists as well as to active Christians and Muslims, all of whom on occasion need calling out. If the book provokes us to a more intentional balance of our *civic duty* with our respective visions – be it a humanist utopia, Christian kingdom or Muslim caliphate (at its best) – then the book will have done its job and we can stop being part of the problem and start being part of the solution.

For secularists, this may require an admission that the premise of their world view owes a debt to the freedoms made available by the Judeo-Christian heritage in western society. For active Christians, it may well mean a greater commitment to *being* 'moral salt' and 'spiritual light' (see Matt. 5:14–16), allowing an interaction that is more rounded, personable, gracious, and faithful to the Christ they commend. For active Muslims, it might be to recognize the scrutiny being placed by western scholarship on the sources of Islam and the text of the Qur'an in the twenty-first century, something the Bible faced in the twentieth century.

I am aware that this is a wide brief to tackle in one book, but that is the point. We are where we are today because different parts of the complex jigsaw are usually considered in isolation from the other parts. All the pieces of the jigsaw are needed to make sense of the picture, which is why I am indebted to a fabulous team of friends and colleagues who are able to view society in an interconnected way. These include British, American and South Asian men and women; they are social practitioners, theologians and academics who pressured me to reframe sections of the book to lose the dross and reveal some gold.

Special thanks to the following who went that extra mile to save me from myself: Ted Bearup (logical thinker and writer), Gillie Goodchild (skilled researcher with an eye for detail), Deborah and Bruce Warren (wise practitioners and transatlantic advisors), and Jay Smith (pioneer debater of those with an Islamist ideology).

By definition, a multicultural society is complex and has layers that are hidden beneath the surface. This is an attempt to peel back the layers, like an onion, to reveal the inner workings of national life. Have I been overambitious by attempting all this in one volume? You decide!

Steve Bell
March 2021

1

And the Problem Is . . .

The rapid changes in western society and how divisions are playing out in public discourse

I have had a problem for forty years!

My problem is the conundrum of why people in all walks of life are more at odds with one another over the presence of Muslims/Islam in the West than any other minority. I notice that some people manage *not* to 'face the facts' about 'dangerous religion' when 'Christians' misbehave, yet they 'fuel the fear' about Muslims when *they* do it. We are clashing with one another over how to respond to such inconsistency.

I often ask myself how we in western societies got to where we are today. What is it about the last hundred years that has caused mega-shifts in society? It seems as if mountains are not only moving, but moving in such a way and at such a speed that they are 'skipping like rams' (see Ps. 114:4 NKJV). Most westerners now embrace, in law, five social equalities, including those of race, gender, age, religion and sexual orientation. What is it about the last century that has changed our societies from being mostly *mono*cultural to becoming *multi*cultural? Also, why are such 'organized' societies still struggling to sort out the implications of these shifts?

The answer may be that western societies were not prepared for the shifts because they were driven by factors partly beyond their control. This left them in a state of disarray with some important underlying issues, which create blockages in the national discourse and feed the social turbulence we face today.

Society seems to be riven with minority interest groups which champion the issues of our time, such as the environment (Extinction Rebellion), or gender (the Me Too movement), or ethnicity (Black Lives Matter), or sexuality (LGBTQ+), or science (the 'new atheism'), or hyper-democracy (the 'woke' culture), or tribal politics (populism), and not least, politicized religion (the Christian kingdom and the Islamic caliphate). I am referring here to the clash of *ultra*-conservative Christians and Muslims.

In the past, the 'battle lines' used to be drawn between one minority and another, or else between a minority group and wider society, such as the campaign for same-sex marriage in 2013. However, times change, and the new battle line has shifted into the minority groups themselves. People who are supposed to be on the same side are now at odds with one another, such as the gay community in tension over some aspects of 'transgenderism', which they are challenging alongside others in wider society. In the same way, 'people of colour' are at odds with one another about what 'structural racism' really means, and they too work with others to have a voice about issues such as 'white fragility'. Similarly, many Christians are at odds with one another about Islam and how to interact with Muslims, just as many Muslims are at odds with their fellow Muslims about Christianity and how to interact with Christians.

A book could be written about each one of the above examples, but this book will mention other minorities only in passing, as a way of focusing on the shift from the former Christian tension *with* Muslims, to Christian versus Christian infighting *about* Muslims; and the Muslim versus Muslim equivalent.

If I have a personal 'angle' in all this, it is that much of what I say is part of my lived experience. I also have a lifelong vocation to support the 'human right' of people with a Muslim family background to flourish in *every* sense – in spirit, mind, emotions. I believe this is only possible when they, like me, have the opportunity, to hear, understand and respond to the good news about Jesus Christ in ways that are not constricted by institutional Christianity and are therefore more appropriate for them.

The core proposition of this book is that Muslim/Christian interaction (at least in the West) inevitably happens in the context of a particular social climate; this means that Christians and Muslims, like everyone else, find themselves picking their way through a lot of debris in that society, like crossing a social minefield. This is the context described by the Old Testament prophet Isaiah, who calls us to 'prepare the way' for righteousness and justice. He says: 'Every mountain [*shall* be] made low' and 'rough ground *shall* become level' (Isa. 40:3–4).[1] Surely this is precisely what we need in our multicultural western society where the issue is *not* just about race and faith, but also about many subcultures based on other things.

To 'prepare the way' in society may sound simple, but it is not. When we persist in it, we may provoke the occasional explosion in our social minefield. This may throw us off our feet, but it is 'par for the course'. For me, such explosions have come more from my fellow Christians than from others, but I take heart in the knowledge that my Muslim counterparts, who are 'preparing the way' in their own community, experience the same thing from their well-meaning fellow Muslims.

I first wrote about my lifelong vocation in the book *Grace for Muslims?*, which tells the story of my adventures living in the Middle East throughout the 1980s.[2] At that time, I must confess I had a bad attitude towards Muslims and Islam, an attitude I thought was *normal*. It proved to be unnecessary and unhelpful, and when I resettled in the West after a decade, I felt I had acquired a more nuanced view. However, by now some people considered me *abnormal* – particularly those in evangelical Christian circles at the time. One well-known Christian minister asked if I was secretly of Muslim descent myself. This implied he thought I had become 'infected', as if the Islamic faith were a disease, not a heritage. Other active Christians assumed I had gone 'soft' on Muslims and Islam, or that I was becoming theologically 'liberal' (a term used as a slur in evangelical 'cancel culture'). In case you are wondering: no, I do not have Muslim relatives, though my family tree *does* go back to Senegal in Islamic West Africa. To imagine that Islam is somehow 'catching' like a spiritual infection seems closer to the Pharisaic rules about *ritual purity* than to a rational understanding.[3] This is an example of an attempt to hold a discriminatory view and to conceal it in a cloak of theological respectability that it does not deserve. We will see more on this in chapter 5 because it is technically 'racist'.

My personal paradigm-shift in the Middle East came about because I realized my attitude was based on limited information that was skewed by prejudice, bias and stereotype. It was a working theory that had to give way to fresh information based on first-hand experience – a process I will enlarge on in chapter 7. To be fair, *some* of my earlier assumptions were valid, but a lot were *not*. I realized that I was part of the problem rather than part of the solution, which is true of many western Christians today. This is the 'problem' I mentioned at the top of this chapter.

If anything, it seems this problem has got *worse* in the current climate, because people are more vociferous than ever. They seem to agree to disagree, but they do so disagreeably. I am not suggesting there are no 'issues' regarding the Muslim communities in the West; there are, but many of them are the same as for black or other racial neighbourhoods. I will be focusing on what is more particular to Muslim communities – not to single them out or suggest an 'us and them' scenario in matters that are not necessarily their fault, but rather to help other minority groups and wider society understand what 'everyday' Muslims face and how they may be feeling about things, and what Muslims and active Christians can do (even together) to 'prepare the way'.

Some issues are inevitable when immigrant individuals and families transplant themselves from the East into the West. The point here is that we need an accurate grasp of the issues, and a healthy and wise way of responding to them, rather than wasting time and energy (as much media coverage does) *reacting* to peripheral issues that become 'paper tigers'. This is to 'strain out a gnat but swallow a camel' (Matt. 23:24). When we recognize what some of the *underlying* issues are, it helps us avoid having unnecessarily strident reactions. We will return to this in chapter 7.

This negative narrative is an understandable and natural response to events such as 9/11 in the USA and 7/7 in the UK, as well as the Arab Spring, the rise and decline of ISIS, the eruption of Islamist violence in the Middle East, the ongoing terrorist atrocities in Europe, and the lava flow of refugees seeking sanctuary in the West.

However, we have not been helped by the sloppy reporting of a 'religiously illiterate' western media, nor by the inept handling of some western governments. As a result, the onlooker has been left to form conclusions about *all* Muslims, and so the damage has been done and we are still picking through the debris in public discourse. The *surface* issues remain the violent and bullying behaviour of a *minority* of Muslims, and the issues have become turbocharged and polarized to the point where (at least for me) addressing them is like licking your finger and sticking it into a live electrical socket. We are in desperate need of leaders (political, media and faith-based) who will champion the cause as we 'prepare the way' together.

Below, I outline two extreme views of Muslims in order to highlight and illustrate the Christian/Christian tension that exists in our society today.

The Conciliatory View

Some Christians see Muslims and Islam as the living embodiment of the ancient Semitic world. For them, Islam is a significant, Torah-based religion that regulates every aspect of life and causes the devout to live in ways that are not a million miles away from the spirit and observance of hasidic Judaism. For them, it is significant that the ancient Gulf Jews, at the time of Islam's founding, used the word 'Allah' to refer to the God of Abraham, and therefore they saw Jehovah and Allah as the same referent (i.e. the same being). For them, like Christianity (at least in its conservative evangelical expression), Islam is a 'missionary' movement which has the same tendency towards triumphalism and the same belief that its followers are custodians of

God's final message to humanity, which is seen as the solution for the ills of the world.[4]

Conciliatory Christians are prepared to look beyond the sense of competition with Christianity, and even the threat of political violence posed by a minority of Muslims, in order to see the potential of devout and fair-minded Muslims to be moral reinforcements enriching the fabric of western society. In this sense, Muslims are like the Samaritan traveller whom Jesus made the hero of a parable – they model the Judeo-Christian view that human beings cannot 'live by bread alone' (see Matt. 4:4) and that society is not just about the 'standard of living' but also the 'quality of life'. This view does not see Muslims as the problem, let alone 'the enemy'.

From the conciliatory viewpoint, if (as some argue) the Islamic tradition inflicted onto the world Usama bin Laden and his like, it is only fair to also say that, in a similar way, Christendom arguably inflicted Adolf Hitler and his like onto the world. It is about having a *fair* and *balanced* assessment of how the world has worked so far.

The Combative View

This view is the polar opposite of the conciliatory view. It is sceptical of everything and embraces what could be called a 'hermeneutic of suspicion'. For instance, it sees Allah not as an aberration of the Judeo-Christian tradition but as a 'false god'. Proponents of this view point to some fairly compelling *surface* facts, such as that most refugees to the West are fleeing Islamic countries; and they ask why most religious violence in the world is committed by Muslims (NB: mostly against their fellow Muslims). This view cites issues in the news, such as the taped evidence given at trial by people such as Abu Hamza al-Masri who said that the British are 'living in a toilet . . . like animals' and that 'no drop of liquid is more loved by Allah than blood', and, 'If we do not use terrorism or torture, what are we going to use?'[5] This sort of extreme rhetoric becomes the lens through which members of the media, not to mention conspiracy theorists, see Muslims and then encourage a negative narrative of Muslims/Islam. For them, Islamic violence is evidence of a global 'medieval death-cult' which is driven by a holy text that is bent on world domination like a spiritual form of communism; but this claim is true of only a *fraction* of Muslims and does not define most Muslims, who become tarred with the same brush as the psychotic fringe.

We will see in chapter 8 why those on the lunatic fringe are as they are, and that many fair-minded Muslims are as concerned about it as others are. Part of my problem is how little the media notice and report the Muslim who does the 'Good Samaritan' thing, showing advanced citizenship by doing impressive random acts of kindness for the public good.

To avoid becoming naively *pro* or paranoiacally *anti* in such issues, we need both an impartial attitude and a sufficient number of reliable facts; I will refer to this as the need for both 'grace' and 'truth'. I have friends who are becoming either *ultra*-conciliatory or *ultra*-combative; to do this they have to be increasingly impervious to any facts that do not affirm their prior conclusions. The ultra-conciliatory view fails to account for the dark underbelly of 'dangerous religion' that is so evident in certain expressions of Christianity and Islam, let alone think of calling them out for it. Likewise, the ultra-combative view fails to account for any redeeming features in a religion (I'm thinking of Islam here) which could be recognized and affirmed as a contribution to the common good in society.

This closed-mindedness is present at each end of a spectrum of opinion on which we can all be placed. My own position is where I believe we all should be, namely somewhere in the middle. This is one fence we do well to sit on and is not a matter of indecision, or a lack of conviction; rather, it is grasping the fact and the fiction about both views. The aim of this book is to show how we can achieve a balance between *naivety* and *hostility*, and between *complacency* and *panic*.

When human nature is faced with a complex problem, it tends to gravitate towards a solution that is as simple as possible, which is why a *good* caricature can help accentuate reality to achieve better clarity about the issues involved in a complex problem. The danger is that unless we take into consideration *all* available facts, we may think we have grasped the whole picture while only having part of it. This point is captured well by an ancient story, retold by Idries Shah in his helpful book, *Elephant in the Dark*:

> A group of blind men heard that a strange animal, called an elephant, had been brought to town, but none of the blind men were aware of its shape and form. Out of curiosity, they said: 'We must inspect it by touch, of which we are capable.' So, they sought it out, and when they found it, they groped around it. The hand of the first man landed on the trunk, so he said: 'This being is like a thick snake.' Another man touched its ear, which seemed like a kind of fan. Another one touched its leg and said: 'The elephant is a pillar like a tree-trunk.' Another blind man placed his hand on its side and said: 'The elephant is a wall.' Another felt its tail and said: 'It's a rope.' The last man felt its tusk and said: 'The elephant is hard and smooth like a spear.'[6]

The story attempts to describe how people of different religions describe God.[7] Shah was a senior Sufi Muslim leader who originally used it to address the disconnect between eastern and western ways of thinking, and the interaction of Christians and Muslims in particular. In his day, Shah reached out, both through his writing and personal friendships, to help westerners grasp that there are several facets to Muslims/Islam, which I will refer to as the 'house of Islam'.[8] Shah's point is the point made above – that a significant section of the house of Islam is 'moderate' (his term, not mine); by this he means moderate in *tone* and behaviour when interacting with non-Muslims.

Shah's use of the elephant story speaks directly to the problem I am describing. The moral of the story is that we should step back and recognize the *whole* (of anything) before zooming in to touch any one facet of it. For example, when a Christian looks at Islam it is possible to touch the:

- 'devout' facet, from which we might conclude that all Muslims are religious

- 'propagating' facet, from which we might conclude that all Muslims are plotting to take over
- 'scholarly' or 'reflective' facet, from which we might conclude that all Muslims know their holy texts
- 'Millennial' or 'younger' facet, from which we might conclude that all Muslims are secular
- 'migrant' or 'diaspora' facet, from which we might conclude that Muslims plan to 'out-birth' us
- 'jihadi' violent facet, from which we might conclude that all Muslims are violent
- 'progressive' or 'forward-looking' facet, from which we might conclude that all Muslims are fair-minded.

If we reverse the allegory above, we could imagine a handful of Muslims being asked to meet one Christian each. Imagine their impression if one Muslim met a member of an Amish community from the USA, another met a Greek Orthodox from Cyprus, another met a Pentecostal from Nigeria, another met a Dutch Reformed person from the Netherlands, and the last Muslim met a member of the English Defence League (a right-wing racist group which claims 'Christian' roots). Now imagine the debriefing session when the Muslims came together to describe Christianity, solely based on their different meetings. Surely they would wonder whether the people they had met were from the same faith at all. Can non-Muslims extend the same courtesy to Muslims and realize that there is a similar variety of Muslim 'types', from the benign to the belligerent?

Wherever you feel your personal view fits on this spectrum, I hope you keep reading because we are about to analyse the social climate that we all share, and to ascertain its effect on Muslims and non-Muslims alike and how we can all 'up our game'. May we all feel less threatened by people who disagree with us, in the knowledge that they are not necessarily *wrong* or ill-intentioned. They are simply touching a different part of the elephant.

2

The Right to Write

The search for social cohesion and whether Christians and Muslims are helping or hindering

It is not the mountain we conquer but ourselves.

Attributed to Edmund Hillary

In this chapter we start to set out the underlying issues in a multicultural society that cause disagreement about Muslims/Islam. We will identify some of the important changes in the world since the colonial era, and why this laid a foundation for the negative narrative about those Muslims who are now living in our postcode in the West.

Most writers (this one included) will tell you they write because they feel compelled to do so. I am writing on this topic because I am a 'person of colour' and therefore part of the visible minority in western societies. I am occasionally mistaken for a Muslim – not least by Muslims – and I grew up in an immigrant family with roots in the Global South. I am an active Christian and so, like Muslims, I am part of a faith community. I am therefore reflecting on forty years of engagement with the issues at hand, including living in the Muslim world, liaising at Westminster with parliamentarians, and interacting with mosque and church faith leaders – not to mention the faith-based mission and development sector.

My background sensitizes me to the issues playing out in society, for instance weird conversations in the public domain, such as happened one morning when I woke up to my bedside radio alarm and heard the BBC's Radio 4 *Today* programme.[1] The voice of the veteran presenter Nick Robinson was beckoning me out of slumber and into consciousness as he interviewed Trevor Phillips, a former head of the UK government's Equalities Commission. Phillips has become a controversial figure for some, and his latest debacle was to be suspended from the Labour Party for alleged 'racism' and 'Islamophobia'. This grabbed my attention because both men seemed to be talking past each other about Muslims/Islam. It was a classic example of the blockage in our public discourse.

As the interview progressed, I had to ask myself if I was the only one who was spotting the double irony in the allegation against Phillips. First, he is of Caribbean descent (which does not mean he is *not* racist, of course); and second, as a public servant, Phillips helped bring the word 'Islamophobia' out of obscurity and into popular use. He also lobbied in favour of the Racial and Religious Hatred Act of 2006 as well as the Equalities Act of 2010. Both pieces of legislation protect all people of faith, including Muslims. Yet here was Phillips being vilified as both a racist and an Islamophobe – the very things his working life had been against.

Regardless of whether you think Phillips is one of the 'good guys' who simply gets accosted by the liberal left, or whether you see Phillips as one of the 'bad guys' who is a right-wing stooge, the interview was flawed by a thinly veiled agenda on Robinson's part. His line of questioning was *accusative* rather than *enquiring*, and *fault*-finding rather than *fact*-finding. Suffice it to say, at this point, that the unstated agenda on Robinson's part revealed a pervasive blockage to what most fair-minded people would call 'healthy' public discourse. It was as if Phillips was being set up for vilification by an interview where he was told what he meant, then asked why he meant that, and his answers were dismissed by citing the 'proof' of his guilt, namely that he had been accused by and then suspended from the Labour Party (the assumption being that the party was right and its actions just).

Later it was revealed that the Labour Party itself was censured by an official inquiry into the harbouring and protecting of racists in its top ranks. We will return in chapter 6 to analyse how the 'high priests' of a repressive form of political correctness are being used to vilify and 'cancel' people as a way of controlling the conversation and deflecting attention away from themselves and onto people they may not like. Phillips' alleged 'crime' was to state in an article that 'Muslims are *different*' (i.e. there are specific cultural and racial variables in their lives and communities).

In the interest of reason, surely we would all hope that a Muslim *is* 'different', in the same way that a practising Christian hopes to be different (i.e. distinctive in ways which society will either welcome or not). For three decades, 'difference' has been celebrated as one of the cornerstones of multiculturalism (see more in chapter 6). The point here is that, whether you have heard of Trevor Phillips or not, and whether you are a fan or not, at least he remained patient and polite when he pointed out to his assertive interviewer that commenting on Muslim community distinctives cannot be 'racist' because Islam is a 'religion', not a 'race'. I had to agree with Phillips on this point. The term 'Christian' tells us nothing about someone's race; he or she could come from anywhere in the world. It also seems illogical to assume that when someone makes an observation about a Muslim's lifestyle, that person is being 'anti-Islamic'. To many people this may be self-evident, but this is not so with the zealots of political correctness who lurk everywhere, including among Nick Robinson's bosses in senior management at the BBC, according to the veteran BBC broadcaster John Humphrys.[2] We will return to the issues of race and faith in chapter 5.

Until the 1990s such issues had not entered the national conversation – it is that recent. Yet in two decades such issues have shot up the agenda in the West. These days, 'everyday' Muslims and mainstream Islam are frequently caught up in a social ferment that is not always of their making. It seems that no one (including fair-minded Muslims) is quite sure what to do about it. People of faith (especially active Christians) are well placed to play a key role as 'peacemakers' who can help interpret the needs of ordinary Muslims to the likes of secular politicians and media, even though (in my experience) they can come under fire themselves for doing so.

Take, for instance, a friend of mine – Toby Howarth, who is the Anglican bishop of Bradford and holds a PhD in a facet of Islam. Bishop Toby gets invited to speak publicly about Islam and Christian interaction. When he does so, he prefers to take off his shoes – not so much as a sign of cultural or religious respect (unless it is in a mosque of course) but more as a visible sign that he will inevitably tread on someone's toes, as the issue is fraught with the potential for misunderstanding. We live in a religiously illiterate society, so it is little wonder that mistakes are made by the press, on social media, or in government departments and local authorities, not to mention by some faith leaders.

All the above is causing active Muslims and Christians to be reticent about talking publicly, let alone with each other. It is all too easy to scurry back behind closed doors to talk *about* the other, rather than *to* them, which is how conspiracy theories get started. It is time to move away from merely cursing the darkness of the unknown, and to turn on the light, for others to see by, and for 'social cohesion' to begin to flourish.

Social Cohesion

In western nations, 'social cohesion' has become a felt need and a government goal of social policies. But let us be clear here that social cohesion is *not* the same thing as *cultural* cohesion. The latter refers to 'assimilation', which is what happens in China where the cultural or religious heritage of ethnic minorities, such as Uyghur Muslims, is forcibly obliterated. The idea of *assimilation* is forced rather than voluntary, while the idea of *cohesion* is the process whereby everyone is invited to include themselves (including their faith and culture), becoming a multicultural facet of the one society.

Social cohesion only works when a society agrees on shared values, and, as we will see later, the Judeo-Christian heritage fits the bill well as a platform which those of other faiths and cultures seem to accept: it lets them know what is required to belong, and it acts as a basis on which to embrace not only the social *rights* that society confers on us but also the social *responsibilities* that we all have. The Judeo-Christian heritage is roughly based on the key biblical texts, including the Law of Moses (a shorthand for the Torah) and the Beatitudes of Christ (a shorthand for the teaching of Jesus and his apostles). The blockage here is that the Judeo-Christian heritage is resisted or even rejected by atheists, secularists and repressive, politically correct (PC) zealots. It can also be conspired against by some sectors of society, which is confusing to immigrant people of faith, many of whom were attracted to the West by the Judeo-Christian moral and spiritual underpinning of western societies.

Social cohesion for people of faith

The Judeo-Christian heritage fosters social justice, as modelled in the biblical vision of *shalom* (rendered as *salam* in Arabic as mainstream Muslims would understand it). When a Jew says '*Shalom aleichem*' or a Muslim says '*Salam alaikum*', they are both referring to the concept of *wholeness* and *well-being*, either of an individual, a family or a community. *Shalom/salam* is about enjoying right relationship with the land we live in (i.e. environmentally), with our neighbour (i.e. relationally), with the community or city (socially), with our country (nationally) and with God (i.e. spiritually).

The prophet Jeremiah puts the onus for this on us all; it is a civic duty where we seek 'the peace and prosperity of the city . . . because if it prospers, you too will prosper' (Jer. 29:7). Many secular politicians may not realize it, but the terms 'social cohesion' or 'social integration' are in accord with this biblical concept, and (in my view) the very terms have come about because our culture is so saturated with the Judeo-Christian heritage as a subconscious frame of reference.

I rarely meet a Muslim, Hindu or Sikh who is not willing to embrace a *dual loyalty* whereby they are willing to 'Give to Caesar what is Caesar's and to God what is God's' (see Mark 12:17). Walter Brueggemann has defined social cohesion as a society that models 'steadfast love' (*hesed* in Hebrew), which promotes 'solidarity' and the inclusion of social 'justice' (i.e. right sharing of resources) and 'righteousness' (i.e. investing in communal well-being).[3] The presence of everyday Muslims makes this more possible, not less so.

Social cohesion for the secularist

For those of no faith, there is a secular definition of social cohesion, namely: 'the ongoing process of developing well-being, a sense of belonging, and voluntary social participation of the members of society, while developing communities that tolerate and promote a multiplicity of values and cultures and granting at the same time equal rights and opportunities in society'.[4] For some, these terms have become a lazy shorthand for a *quiet life*; however, I will be using the terms in a much fuller way which has two aspects.

1. The first is temporal (earthly) and is the need for a public commitment to the 'prosperity of the city' so that all citizens, whether of faith or not, are encouraged to uphold common values such as social justice, corporate responsibility, human freedoms, mutual respect and the sense of civic duty (the things that are Caesar's).
2. The second is eternal (spiritual); for example, it is the calling of Christians to be authentic witnesses by making Jesus' last command our first priority (the things that are God's).

Both these aspects are blocked by obstacles that stand like a mountain range, which must and *can* be moved. It is possible to be aware of these blockages as discrete obstacles in current affairs, without stepping back to appreciate that the obstacles are interconnected to form a mountain range that is bringing society to a halt on the road to *the common good*.

An example of these obstacles is immigration. This first became significant in the UK during the post-war era when the Nationality Act of 1948 was passed, opening the door to economic migrants (my father included) who were invited to fill the gaps in the workforce and help rebuild the country after the Second World War (see more in chapter 7).

To put it mildly, that 'discomfort' in the nation prompted this journey in search of the holy grail we call 'social cohesion'. We now know that this is not likely to be achieved by politely ignoring the 'differences' of any minorities (particularly those of race, faith and culture); rather, the way forward is to ascertain what those differences *are* and account for them in an open, practical and courteous way. In my view, the multicultural experiment has failed because of three things: first, the polite tendency to try to airbrush out the differences; second, the secular assumption that other faiths can be domesticated in the same way that Christianity has been, by being restricted to private expression in places of worship but resisted in 'public space'; and third, that for 'people of faith', religion is a matter of identity, lifestyle, values and a sense of belonging in community. The complexity comes when there are *multiple* communities living side by side. This changes the goalposts of social cohesion because it must be *multidirectional.*

This became apparent to me when my wife was deputy head teacher in an inner-city academy in Birmingham. She witnessed first-hand the occasional social friction when Pakistani and Bangladeshi pupils or their families clashed with one another. For example, Hindu and Muslim youngsters would be at odds due to treating their religious affiliations like opposing football teams, or when a Hindu teenage boy eloped with a Muslim girl; in the latter case a press blackout was ordered by the police to avoid community disturbance over the issue.

Another obstacle to the common good is the presence of strident groups on all sides. For example, as a person of colour I found myself caught up in a protest by the far-right white group known as the English Defence League (EDL), who were vociferously protesting over the ghettoization of some Muslim neighbourhoods by vigilante groups of Muslim youths who were trying to turn them into Muslim-only 'no-go' zones. When a balanced assessment of the situation was offered by Bishop Michael Nazir-Ali (himself of a Pakistani family background), he became a hate target of the 'liberal left', who accused him of racism and Islamophobia (see more in chapter 6).[5] This illustrates the fact that multicultural western societies sit on 'tectonic plates' which periodically rub together, causing earth tremors. The recent deaths of black people in the USA at the hands of the police are a prime example of tremors that can turn into minor earthquakes.

Over the past few centuries, the earthquakes have created an invisible mountain range in the national psyche. This mountain range has shaped the UK's social landscape and social climate in ways that are every bit as real as the country's physical geography.

I am using the geographical metaphor of mountains because it came to me in a dream.

I Have a Dream

I have had few notable dreams in my life, but two of them stand out because they have proved life-changing. The first was a vivid 'night dream' in 1991 where I saw myself attending a gathering in a Christ-centred worshipping community.[6] More than two thirds of the group were people from Muslim families in various parts of the world. Some were asylum seekers, others were settled immigrants, and the rest were indigenous white Britons. This dream occurred fourteen years before the recent migrant-flow, which did not begin until around 2015. Since the dream, I have walked into several such gatherings in the UK and various other countries, including Kurdish Iraq, and all of them have come into being since the 1990s.

The second dream was a 'waking dream' (i.e. a 'daydream') in 2019. In that dream my mind became like a cinema screen with an image that took me back to a place I once visited in the Himalayan mountains of north India in 1990. The scene was of a crisp, clear, brilliantly sunny winter's morning with a cloudless blue sky and snow on the majestic peaks. My attention was drawn to seven mountaintops, which reminded me of the Jewish menorah (seven-branched candlestick). I recognized the central dominant peak as Mount Everest. Its peak was the tallest and had a split top, which made the summit look like a lopsided 'M', standing tall and proud as the jewel in a regal tiara that was worthy of the Raj and empire. On either side of the central twin-peak were five lesser peaks, three on one side and two on the other. The sense I got from the scene was that the Himalayan range is a natural barrier, and it has to be navigated in the same way as the invisible social mountain range in western societies today that is a blockage to healthy interaction between non-Muslims and Muslims (many of whom have family heritage in the British Raj).

The seven peaks in the dream had names, which came instantly to mind as clearly as if they had been labelled. The names indicated the type of obstacle each peak posed. The names of the peaks have become the titles of the remaining chapters of this book, as follows.

Mount Imperial (see chapter 3)

Mount Imperial speaks of the deep-seated assumptions embedded in the legacy of a prestigious colonial past. This peak makes many people (especially those over the age of 60) prone to the 'unconscious bias' of white male superiority. Our ways are 'normal', while 'other' ways need adjectives to qualify them, for example 'Italians are emotional', or 'Americans are brash', or 'Japanese take lots of photos' – but compared to what?

Mount Hegemony (see chapter 4)

Mount Hegemony is the shorter of the twin peaks and is joined at the hip with Mount Imperial. Hegemony is having the 'clout' to exercise pervasive influence over others via cultural, military and/or economic

power – all gained as a legacy of empire. Hegemony tends to assume
it is in the right and that 'the end justifies the means'. This may be an
unconscious bias, but it is seen clearly by any Muslim who was born
on the wrong side of hegemony.

Mount Ethnos (see chapter 5)

Mount Ethnos is linked to, and builds on, the influence of imperialism and hegemony. Mount Ethnos speaks of the racism that is
endemic to human nature and therefore found in all cultures. The
western version is expressed through a notional ethnic pecking order,
which is part of the underbelly of imperialism and cultural hegemony. A significant number of Muslims in the West are black African
or West Indians who have converted to Islam, which has a bearing as
they are part of the debate about the Black Lives Matter movement.

Mount Correct (see chapter 6)

Mount Correct speaks of 'political correctness', which is seen by
some as the 'knight in shining armour' that is here to help victims
of Mount Ethnos. However, as well as protecting ethnic minorities,
it also has the capacity to patronize people and provoke more racism;
for instance, when politically motivated Muslims play the PC system
by using the 'race' and 'Islamophobia' card to further an agenda, their
actions tend to provoke bad feeling against all Muslims.

Mount Strident (see chapter 7)

Mount Strident speaks of the backlash caused by frustration over
political correctness. People are rebelling, insisting on their 'right'
to say what they really think about issues such as race, religion,

immigration, Islam, sexuality, or the European Union. This sense of repressed grievance is really about a loss of freedom of expression.

The result has been damage to the national conversation, because strident Christian voices have joined in to hit out against Muslims/Islam, warning about Islamization, radicalization, Muslims out-birthing white people in order to take over, and so on. The search is on for a better way to express such concerns accurately and appropriately.

Mount Occlusion (see chapter 8)

Mount Occlusion is about the blockages that could trigger a 'heart attack' within the house of Islam. The reasons include a proliferation of 'progressive' views calling for reform; an unprecedented number who are abandoning Islam; Islamist violence driving millions out of their birth countries to seek refuge and asylum in the 'Christian' West; and scholarly questions about the reliability of Islamic history and the Qur'anic text. This is an historic shift!

Mount Mission (see chapter 9)

Too many Christians waste time and energy fighting one another about their 'message', their 'method' and the nature of Muslims/Islam. Mount Mission seems to be the cumulative effect of all the other mountains. The western mission enterprise (local church and mission agencies) is rooted in *western* history, culture, theology, scholarship and structures, which are unconsciously shaped by the legacy of Christendom. As a result, Christians form different theological 'tribes' and disagree with one another over issues such as:

• what the irreducible and non-negotiable elements of the 'gospel' are (i.e. what is to be conveyed)

- the nature and desired outcomes of the Great Commission of Christ (i.e. what 'good' looks like)
- the nature of Islam, for example to what extent it is predicated on ancient Judaism
- what is biblically permissible in Christian witness among Muslims
- what conversion and discipleship looks like for people of another culture and religion
- how cautious to be about the restrictions imposed on Christian witness by political correctness.

Such questions form an obstacle to a united approach and lessen the likelihood of a Muslim encountering the good news about Jesus.

Grace Pass (see chapter 10)

The last thing I noticed about the mountain range was that there was 'a way' through it, namely Grace Pass. Like most dreamlike impressions, this aspect was a bit like sci-fi, because it was possible to navigate *over* the mountain range, as well as *through*, or *around*, or even *underneath* it, a bit like walking through a brick wall. Whichever route one took, 'the way' had already disarmed the ability of the mountains to be a blockage any more. The mountains became navigable – as obstacles shifted.

Mountains Can Move

The reality we see today is that obstacles are indeed shifting, so, amid the bad news of our times, there are also some encouraging green shoots. Take, for instance, a global prayer awakening among active Christians who are praying for the spiritual well-being of Muslims, especially during the annual fasting month of Ramadan and the annual week of Haj.[7] A lesser-known fact is that this concerted prayer has been going on in parallel with the rise in the numbers of Jews and Muslims who are changing their heart allegiance to Jesus Christ as their Messiah – which is a different thing from embracing *institutional* Christianity.

Another lesser-known fact is that during their daily formal prayer, millions of devout Muslims petition God with the words: 'Lead us in *the right way*.'[8] Unbeknown to them, Jesus said: 'I am *the way* and the truth and the life. No one comes to the Father except through me' (John 14:6). Jesus Christ is Grace Pass personified to the Muslim people encountering him.

Meanwhile on the Ground

There are some heady issues in this dream. It can seem detached from our current reality and a long way from the visible world as we know it. However, if it is a 'prophetic' insight, its caveat may well be: 'the revelation awaits an appointed time . . . Though it linger, wait for it; it will certainly come and will not delay' (Hab. 2:3). In the meantime we can be reassured that, as the issues surrounding the mountain range become more navigable for us all, we can expect a positive trickle-down effect to local situations where change is indeed happening, even though it is almost imperceptible at times.

A case in point is my own local church, which opened up its minor hall for a halal Christmas meal for the men of the local mosque. I sat next to two unrelated men of Gujarati family background. One was in his late thirties and the other a retiree. As we chatted away, enjoying one another's company, they surprised me by describing separate holidays they had taken which included a trip to the Vatican. Their families had both gone there out of sheer curiosity and the desire to 'see how the other half lived'. How times change!

We turn now to examine the implications of the first mountain blockage – Mount Imperial, which is possibly the most foundational of all and, because of what it is, affects both Muslims, Christians and people of no faith alike. What is Mount Imperial? Why does it affect both Muslims and non-Muslims alike? How can society navigate it?

3

Mount Imperial

Colonialism and the impacts of its legacy on the thinking of Muslims and Christians

> If our history fails to convey the truth about the past,
> how can we live truthfully in the present?
>
> J. Ingleby[1]

In this chapter we describe the deep-seated psychological legacy of empire and the unconscious bias it has created towards white male superiority. We identify some things that white and South Asian Britons have in common, due to their shared history. We follow the development of Christendom and how empire led to 'institutional Christianity', how it affected our understanding of Jesus' teaching, and how it hampers interaction with those who are racially, culturally or religiously different from us.

The British people are conflicted about the British Empire. Some point to a laudable history (usually written by British historians) that has left a lasting contribution in the countries involved, such as the creation of a reliable and well-run infrastructure, including transport, communication, education systems, the rule of law, and civil administration.

Others claim that any benefit was eclipsed by a dark underbelly of predatorial supply-chains, such as those that existed when Britain sent gunboats into Hong Kong to ensure the free trade of its Indian-grown opium, the production of which it had commandeered in order to take over the Chinese opium industry. In addition to taking over India's opium production, Britain crippled India's competitive textile industry, forcing Indians to buy British-made textiles, made from cotton picked by African slaves and shipped to Britain to be woven into textiles to be sold to India, to strengthen Britain's conquest of the opium market in China.[2]

This view argues that even Adolf Hitler built infrastructure to benefit the Third Reich. This may help explain why the British Empire left a mixture of positive 'heritage', as well as the negative 'baggage' we will focus on in this chapter. It may seem a strange connection to make, but the former British Empire has become a blockage to healthy interaction between non-Muslims and people of Muslim heritage, now living together in the West.

What is it about western nations that makes them think history is always on their side? Perhaps it is because history is usually written by those who came out on top at the time. We certainly tend to read what westerners say about it. I must point here to Jonathan Ingleby who is a refreshing exception because he urges us to 'interpret *the sweep* of history'.[3] When we do so, we find that empire usually causes an imperialist nation to become an earthly expression of the 'powers of darkness' (see Eph. 6:12). This may come as a shock, but on the continent of Europe, it happened as societies moved from being 'sacralist' to 'secularist' (i.e. from a sacred to a secular frame of reference) and from the power of monarchies to that of commercial corporations.

A downside of colonialism (at home and overseas) is that it can impact a national psyche for generations. For example, we tend to have an imbedded assumption that the English language is superior, along with western laws, values, science and technology. Ingleby rightly identifies the corporate greed of the West, along with our addiction to comfort, consumerism, racial hierarchy and misuse of power. Rather than recognizing this, there is an unconscious bias (particularly in western evangelicals) that transfers the problem upwards to the unseen 'spiritual realm', which they prefer to see as the true 'axis of evil'; or the problem gets consigned forwards to the 'end of the age' (i.e. kicking it into the long grass of the future). The result is a disclaimer that absolves *us* of responsibility for the ills of the world and the need to shine a light on these things.[4]

This blind spot came crashing into my awareness when American friends helped me understand the negative impacts of British colonial behaviour in America. As a Brit, I was oblivious to the fact that Americans were incensed at being subjugated as a colony by the British government and military, which treated them as 'other' and denied them representation in the British Parliament. The flipside to this is the irony that modern America is now doing the same thing when it uses its own power to exert economic, military and cultural clout in the world, failing to recognize that the USA has become a de facto empire which is policing the world with an attitude that says: 'Our way is best.'

Until recently, the 'glory days' of Britain were thought to be when 'the sun never set on the British Empire'. This narrative is now being challenged, and even those in charge of the Queen's honours list are reviewing its medals, such as the Order of the British Empire (OBE), which is now an anachronism. The British blind spot includes the fact that many Muslim countries were either colonies or protectorates of Britain, whose relationship with them transitioned from being paternalistic 'master/servant' as part of an empire, to being 'colleague/ equal' in the British Commonwealth. While Queen Elizabeth II is alive, the Commonwealth remains a softer 'maternal' relationship, but this too may change one day.

As the Islamic nations have made their own way in a post-colonial world, 'political Islam' has emerged on the back of the oil boom of the 1960s, which enabled a more confident Islam to flourish. It seems to me that this may have been the point at which the British view of Muslims/Islam began to be conflicted, as it emerged that not all Muslims are 'cuddly' and some are dangerous. Philip Lewis says that since the British Empire, western nations have tended to see 'other races, cultures and religions as either an ideological threat, or as potential political allies, or trading partners, or as objects of intellectual curiosity. It seems that, only as a last resort, does it tend to see these people as fellow citizens.'[5]

This captures well the effect of three expressions of 'empire': the Roman Empire in Europe, the Near East and the Mediterranean basin; the Moghul Empire across the Indo-Pakistan subcontinent and beyond; and the British Empire, which covered a quarter of the globe. These three empires impacted one another; for instance, past generations of South Asians were subjugated by Muslims in the Moghul Empire, just as white Britons were subjugated by the Roman Empire. These two races have also been part of the same empire – the British Empire (whites as master and South Asians as servant). Neither can we overlook how in the Second World War white Britons fought and died alongside their black and South Asian comrades of the British Empire. British English reflects this shared history in its borrowed words, taken from languages such as Hindi and Arabic; for example, 'bungalow', 'gymkhana', 'shufti', 'bint' and 'algebra'. South Asian curry is thought to be the UK's most popular dish.

The story of empire is therefore part of the colourful tapestry that is the backdrop to life in modern Britain. All this serves to enhance but also complicate the interaction between white non-Muslims and South Asian and black British Muslims today.

Britain in the Roman Empire

For the British, Mount Imperial starts in AD 312 when the Roman general Constantine became emperor of Rome. By AD 380 he had legalized Christianity, which set a new course in European history as Christians were able to move from a position of vulnerability to a share in power.[6] From this point on, there was a tension between the 'earthly empire' and the 'heavenly kingdom' (i.e. between the entitlement of worldly power and the teaching of Jesus). As a response to this tension, Emperor Constantine delayed his own baptism as a Christian, almost until his deathbed. Julyan Lidstone points out that to fully commit to Christ, Constantine had to 'give up the purple', which was the colour of the imperial toga that signified his earthly status.[7]

Did Constantine convert to Christ or was he merely converting Christianity to himself? We cannot know, but what we do know is that the Roman Empire was intact for a thousand years after his time, before being dismantled in stages. The 'Eastern Roman Empire', administered from Constantinople, lasted until AD 1453. Rome itself was overrun in AD 455, and the 'Western Roman Empire', administered from Rome, fell in AD 476. The city of Rome was a leading city of Christendom and was the epicentre of what became western Christianity; and some historians argue that the last vestige of the Roman Empire continued via the imperial family line of Charlemagne to Napoleon Bonaparte in the 1800s.

Christianity in the Roman Empire

The Roman Empire became known as the 'Holy Roman Empire' in AD 800 when Charlemagne was made emperor. Now there was a temporal head, and a pope as a spiritual head. This marked the fusion of 'church' and 'state' and turned Christianity into another colonial religion in the same way as Islam and Zoroastrianism. Some argue that this was the start of the era of 'Christendom' (i.e. the physical domain of Christ) and a Roman church which had access to wealth, position and military power. The church became a religio-political entity which fought wars to create and/or defend 'Christian territory'. This was paralleled in Islam by the fusion of faith and fighting for the Islamic empire (i.e. the caliphate).

To everyone's shame, Christian and Muslim armies mirrored each other in an era when the sword was brandished by both sides.

The Crusader wars were fought; the word 'Crusade' was derived from the Latin *cruce* or 'cross'. As the 'Christian' hymn says, it was:

Onward, Christian soldiers,
Marching as to war,
With the cross of Jesus
Going on before.[8]

So-called 'Christian' armies went out with a cross carried before them and even emblazoned on the uniform.

The prevailing understanding at the time of the Crusades was less: 'Thy kingdom come', and more a human bid to enforce God's kingdom geographically and politically. There was confusion between the 'divine kingdom' and the 'human empire'. This fell way short of Jesus' teaching: 'The kingdom of God is in your midst' (Luke 17:21) and 'My kingdom is *not* of this world. If it were, my servants would fight . . .' (John 18:36). Western nations have tried to solve the tension between 'kingdom' and 'empire' by officially separating church from state, yet to this day many people (i.e. Christians and Muslims) speak as though they are one. At least Muslim states do not try to pretend to separate the two, but justify the caliphate mindset by citing how western nations are still carrying a torch for Christendom. This slips out whenever the West is blamed for military 'interference' in Muslim lands, such as Afghanistan, Iraq and Libya (where it is not wanted), while also being blamed for *not* 'intervening' more, such as in Bosnia (where it was welcomed to protect Muslims).

It may also explain why when a Muslim converts to Christ, he or she tends to be labelled a defector to the religion of colonialists (i.e. the agents of Christendom). This 'us' and 'them' mentality is rooted in an 'unconscious bias' held by Muslims and non-Muslims alike. It assumes that faith and territory are synonymous and that the one is an expression of the other. In a post-Christendom and post-caliphate world, they are not.

The Legacy of Christendom and Caliphate

The people of 'Christian' and 'Muslim' nations are like goldfish, which do not seem to be aware that they swim in water. We have all been in our cultural environment since birth, so, like the fish, we stop being aware of it, which explains why in Britain even secular humanists and atheists will argue from assumptions that are rooted in the Judeo-Christian heritage and are therefore *Christian*. Our cultural waters nurture our view of the world, such as taking a linear view of history as opposed to the cyclical view of the Buddhist and Hindu world.[9] Although buried more deeply in the western psyche, there is the Christendom assumption from history that we are part of the 'upper ones' in the world, that is, the 'haves'. We see this as validated by our political, economic and cultural arrangements, and sadly, it filters through into our theology and church practices in the West. Ken Wilson points out that 'the presence of Jesus Christ is almost external to the forms of Christianity that claim to represent him. He wants his religion back because it could be argued that institutionalized Christianity has become a sort of trademark infringement of the original movement that carried His name'.[10]

Imperialist Assumptions Linger

We can see imperialist assumptions about faith and territory in the world expressed in hymns such as:

Jesus shall reign where'er the sun
Doth his successive journeys run;
His kingdom stretch from shore to shore,
Till moon shall wax and wane no more.[11]

Even the Greenwich Meridian harks back to the days when global time-zones were all calibrated by British time. Eddie Arthur is a former CEO of Wycliffe Bible Translators in the UK and sums this up by pointing out that British people who are over 70 years old are 'children *of* empire', while the rest of us are 'children of the *legacy* of empire' where:

> Vast swathes of the world map were coloured pink . . . where Britain ruled, or had recently ruled. The Empire was already passing, and Britain was in decline; but we hung on to notions of grandeur. We slowly grew to realize that we were no longer what we were. We are a small nation among many on the earth – a reality that we still find hard to grasp. The position of the British church is analogous to the position of the UK in world politics. As we get used to Britain no longer being a dominant economic, political, or military force in the world, so too we need to adjust our expectations about the role of the British church in the world. We need to find our appropriate place within the new ecclesiastical world order. Just like British football, those pesky foreigners have taken Christianity and seem to be doing it better than we do.[12]

Few empires envisage what the world will look like after their demise – the Roman Empire and the British Empire included. The respected scholar Lesslie Newbiggin made a life study of the erosion in British society; this first impacted him when he returned to the UK in 1974 after living in India for nearly forty years. He reflected on the departure from the Christian faith across Europe, which he said caused a 'loss of confidence in its own validity' and triggered a 'disappearance of hope'. Newbiggin saw the continent of Europe as exhibiting 'one of the toughest forms of paganism' which presents 'the greatest intellectual and practical task facing the church'.[13]

How 'Christian' Is a Christian Country?

Since Christendom started to recede into the rear-view mirror of history, it has become harder to say that Britain is a 'Christian' country without qualifying what that now means. According to the last UK national census, 59.3% of Britons identified themselves as 'Christian', which is 33.2 million people.[14] However, respondents would use the word in one of two senses: first, to mean 'culturally' or 'nominally' Christian, and second, in a more religious sense. Evangelicals define a 'Christian' as J.I. Packer did when he said: 'the essence of Christianity is not primarily in belief nor behaviour patterns but in the reality of personal communion here and now with Christianity's living founder, Jesus Christ.'[15]

I said earlier that non-religious Britons tend to agree with the notion of 'cultural' Christianity, as it seems accurate when 'almost everything you touch in British culture, whether its art, its literature, or the English language, all [have] been shaped by the Judeo-Christian tradition, the Bible, the liturgical calendar',[16] and realize that 'nearly all British social institutions have been born in [Christendom] because the idea of society is the soul of [its] religion'.[17] Britain has had a Christian presence since St Augustine first arrived fourteen hundred years ago. Over the centuries, the nation has been shaped around a 'church of state' and, without the biblical framework in society, some doubt that Britain would ever have achieved nationhood, as England did during the reigns of King Henry VIII and Queen Elizabeth I.[18]

The church in the British Isles also weathered the Reformation, the Enlightenment, the Industrial Revolution and two world wars. Yet the relevance of an *established* church is increasingly questioned in the postmodern era as attendance has dropped from 27% in 1900 to a mere 10% in 2000.[19] That said, we should also remember the anecdotal calculation that under normal conditions, there are still more people attending a church on a Sunday morning than those attending a football match on a Saturday afternoon.

Cultural Christianity

'Cultural Christians' are usually happy to engage in the church's rites of passage, including infant baptism, marriage and funerals (i.e. the services of 'hatch, match and dispatch'). The culturally Christian markers in national life include royal weddings, state funerals, and ceremonials such as the Act of Remembrance at the Cenotaph in London, daily prayer before parliamentary business, bishops serving as 'Lords Spiritual' in the House of Lords, and the monarch's coronation oath as defender of the Reformed Christian faith. Culturally Christian people may look to the church to provide pastoral solace to the nation in times of crisis, insecurity or major transition.[20] This is likely to be why cultural Christians like to think they 'belong' to the church, even though they do not 'believe'.[21] My father-in-law is in his nineties and has no personal faith, yet adamantly refers to himself as a 'lay Christian', distinguishing himself from 'churchgoing Christians'. Even some high-profile atheists refer to themselves as 'cultural Anglicans', including scientist Richard Dawkins,[22] historian David Starkey and author Douglas Murray.

We should add a comment on the way the Bible has shaped the English language. For example, even TV newscasters use expressions such as 'going the extra mile', 'made a scapegoat', 'turn the other cheek', 'be a good Samaritan', 'to be a Judas', 'sacrificial lamb', 'it's a cross I have to bear'. The Bible also provided the foundation for law, and concepts such as human rights, individual freedoms, the sanctity of life, and social justice. The historian Tom Holland argues that the Reformation and the Enlightenment were outgrowths of the Judeo-Christian heritage. He even goes so far as to suggest that the more recent revolution in sexual ethics and identity politics is a more liberal phenomenon which could not have happened if it were not for concepts embedded in the Judeo-Christian heritage.[23]

The Search for British Values

It seems that only vestiges of the previous Christendom era survive and that its effects are massively diminished in what many are calling the 'post-Christian era'. However, while the influence of secularism has marginalized *formal* religion, it has not displaced 'spirituality' but merely driven it in different directions.[24] We are now realizing that 'the broader our definition of "faith", the more of it we will find in national life'.[25] Western societies are now home to three categories of people: those who are members of *world faiths*, those of *no faith*, and those who embrace emerging *hybrid belief* systems. All of these live together, which creates a felt need for some common foundation to coalesce around. I am arguing that the Judeo-Christian heritage, which some want to jettison, is the most viable contender, as it provides a 'coherent narrative that is sufficiently robust to give direction and agreed values, for all people of faith and none'.[26] Research shows that, broadly speaking, Britons agree on the following values:[27]

- democracy
- the rule of law
- the responsibility of all people for their actions
- the equality of all people under the law
- freedom of speech and the right to individual conscience, including political and religious convictions
- the right of all men and women to live free from persecution
- to seek the common good
- not to seek personal rights over those of others
- alongside our rights, to keep in view our responsibilities.

These values are not unique to 'Christians' nor are they entirely the property of the Judeo-Christian heritage; however, they are all accounted for within that heritage. Those resisting this list are not the fair-minded people of the minority ethnic and faith groups; indeed, if they did not approve of it, they would not be prepared to live here. Also, it is arguably a courtesy to the majority fair-minded white people, who are also concerned about the prospect of the British Isles one day abandoning what has after all been an historic anchor.

So How Imperialist Am I?

The problem with an unconscious bias (or a blind spot) is that often we are the last person to know we have one. The only way to identify unconscious bias is to monitor behaviour. Here's a test that uncovered one of mine. A boy and his father are driving along and have a dreadful accident. The boy's father dies, but the emergency services rescue the boy and get him to hospital where surgeons are on standby to operate. The lead surgeon comes into the operating theatre, stops, and says: 'I can't conduct this procedure because this boy is my son.' What's going on? I assumed that one of the men was the biological father and the other a stepfather, perhaps by divorce. However, the surgeon was the boy's *mother*. Enough said!

Another example I have seen is that many westerners affirm the saying: 'When in Rome do as the Romans do', but when they go abroad on holiday they become irritated by what the locals do; they often put their angst down to culture shock, but what is 'culture shock' if not a reaction to what does not conform to our deeply rooted expectation about how things should be? When I lived in the Middle East, I noticed western expatriates gravitating to people like themselves and preferably of their own nationality, yet being dismissive when locals behaved in the same way. The same situation plays out in the UK where I have seen a Muslim judged by his or her appearance, and accused of non-compliance with 'British ways', by people who were unaware that the Muslim in question affirmed British ways as much as they did.

This happened to Rageh Omaar, the prominent British journalist whose family heritage is from Somalia, a former British protectorate. He had a relatively privileged British upbringing, including a private education.[28] On paper he had the 'right school tie' and British accent to qualify as a member of the establishment, but like so many Britons with a Muslim family heritage, he was politely categorized as 'other' and not allowed to integrate. This problem is compounded when those who are resistant to British Muslims go on to blame the Muslim for not doing more to integrate. I suggest that this is more than mere racial stereotyping; it is deeply embedded in the historical notion of faith, territory and 'us' and 'them' and who belongs and who does not. Rageh Omaar eloquently captures this predicament when he says: 'No amount of privilege, education, knowledge, or experience could shield me from moments that would be familiar to every young immigrant, and which, since September 11, 2001, would be particularly familiar to British Muslims: being silent while your identity is made by others.'[29]

This is something people of colour can face almost daily. Mount Imperial is aided and abetted by its twin – Mount Hegemony, which derives from imperialism. The two work together to create the blockage to interaction between a non-Muslim and a Muslim. What is 'hegemony', how does it draw strength from imperialism, and how can we navigate it? This is where we go next.

4

Mount Hegemony

Who is in control politically, financially, militarily and theologically?

What's worse than a problem is when we think something is normal.

Attributed to Revd Jesse Jackson[1]

In this chapter we define, describe and explain what hegemony is and how it is the conjoined twin of imperialism. We see how it both draws on and feeds off the colonial mindset. We identify how this can impact both Muslim and Christian by blocking healthy and effective interaction.

The age of empire is over, but it would seem that many people did not get the memo. As a result, we often assume that we are in the 'post-colonial' era, while in reality we are living in a *neo-colonial* era (i.e. under a new form of colonialism). This is because empire continues in the guise of hegemony, which is a by-product of colonization and perpetuates the old paternal patterns but achieves them via the 'clout' of military, economic and cultural power. This is why, in my dream, Mount Hegemony was conjoined with Mount Imperial as the lesser summit of a twin peak.

What Is Hegemony?

The first time I heard the word 'hegemony' was at a gathering of community leaders in the Ghamkol Sharif Mosque in Small Heath, Birmingham. Among the guests was Claire Short MP, who was addressing Muslim and Christian leaders on the topic of the government's holy grail – 'social cohesion' – and how to achieve it. After one of the sessions, I was enjoying a welcome cup of tea with a Muslim leader when he said to me: 'Western hegemony is the problem!' I was stumped by this Pakistani man who had introduced me to an English word I had never heard before. I asked him to define the word and he did his best to explain: 'It is when the chips in society are stacked in someone's favour.' When I got home, I looked it up and found that it comes from the Greek word *hēgemonía*[2] whose root meaning is 'to lead' or 'to rule'. The word 'hegemony' therefore refers to the leadership or rule of one group (i.e. the 'upper ones' I mentioned earlier).

Hegemony builds on the power of imperialism, so nations which have had an empire are more prone to this sort of dominance, but those that are simply *resourceful* are also prone to express it economically, militarily and culturally. Hegemony enters the DNA of the more powerful nations and impedes healthy interaction of the 'haves' with the 'have nots' – the ethnically, culturally or religiously different peoples of less powerful nations. This is compounded when individuals from such nations transfer to the West, where they form ethnic and religious minorities.

Since the dismantling of the British Empire, people from the ends of the earth have come to live in the UK – a process that reminds me of the Star Wars franchise and the film title: *The Empire Strikes Back*. This is what has been happening in the 'neo-colonial' era when the peoples of former colonies and protectorates have come to settle in the former 'motherland'. The social implications of this situation are still being worked through today, which is why you are reading this book.

An important fictional drama was the TV series *Noughts & Crosses*.[3] It portrays the 'empire strikes back' theme by turning colonialism on its head so that a thinly disguised Africa becomes an empire in its own right, and Africans return to the former colonial 'motherland' (a thinly disguised Britain) as colonizers of their former white masters. The new colony is governed by a black elite ruling-class which retains 'token whites' in its lower echelons of law enforcement and the military. The drama unfolds as a Romeo and Juliet romance takes place between a young black woman from a wealthy privileged background and a white youth from a poor, underprivileged servant-class family.

Several white friends of mine told me they were disturbed by the drama and could not cope with the revisiting of empire from the opposite direction. It messed with their head to identify themselves with the experience of being subjugated. Even when powerful nations set out to support weaker nations through aid and development, they may inadvertently create a soft form of hegemony; that is, if the outcome includes political, economic or cultural control. This has also been true of institutions such as the World Bank.[4] In this sense, even 'soft power' can become as pernicious as overt domination.

The blockage of hegemony is as real to a Muslim who merely *senses* it as it is to a Muslim who can pinpoint it and articulate what is going on. For non-Muslims too, it can only help us to realize that this influence is ubiquitous in the western psyche and is how the world works. Like imperialism, hegemony is rooted so deeply it becomes an unconscious bias – that of the 'upper ones'. This is 'cultural myopia', where we subconsciously judge other cultures through the lens of our own. A timely book that is of prophetic significance has been written by Chris Wright; entitled *These Are Your Gods*,[5] it is an exposé of hegemony in both church and state. Wright traces the signs in the individual lives of politicians and church leaders alike, men and women who are being infected by the gods of power, position, popularity, personal gain, success, wealth, influence, nationalism and unaccountability – all of which is antithetical to the kingdom of God and contrary to the way of Jesus and his apostles, who operated with integrity, humility, and *servant* attitude and actions.

Historic Hegemony

There may be a fine line between a healthy sense of national pride and *nationalism*. The debate over hegemony in the national psyche recently focused on the patriotic song 'Rule Britannia', which, after the national anthem, is second only to 'Land of Hope and Glory'. Both are traditionally sung on the last night of the Promenade Concerts ('the Proms') held annually in the Royal Albert Hall, London. Perhaps the sing-along is a light-hearted (if wistful) reminiscence of the bygone days of empire, but the lyrics are as follows:

When Britain first, at heaven's command, arose from out the
   azure main,
This was the charter of the land, and Guardian Angels sang this
   strain:

[*Refrain*] Rule, Britannia! Britannia rule the waves!
Britons never, never, never shall be slaves.

The nations not so blest as thee must in their turn to tyrants fall,

While thou shalt flourish great and free: the dread and envy of
   them all.

Still more majestic shalt thou rise, more dreadful from each foreign stroke,
As the loud blast that tears the skies serves but to root thy native oak.

Thee haughty tyrants ne'er shall tame; all their attempts to bend
   thee down
Will but arouse thy generous flame but work their woe and thy
   renown.

To thee belongs the rural reign; thy cities shall with commerce shine;
All thine shall be the subject main, and every shore it circles, thine.

The Muses, still with freedom found, shall to thy happy coasts
   repair.
Blest isle! with matchless beauty crowned, and manly hearts to
   guard the fair.[6]

Such lyrics may be more about folklore than fact, but they are in
the same category as the notion of the 'bulldog spirit' which helped
Britain steel itself to survive the Blitz. The Britons who were born as
children of the empire tend to feel that, if such a spirit ever existed,
it has dissipated in today's more fragile generation. Alternatively, that
grit may be re-emerging as the other side of the coin, namely the
determination that is expressing itself in a strident reaction to those
who are 'different' due to their race, their culture, their religion, their
dress, and their language – all summed up in people of other faiths.

Theological Hegemony

Hegemony has been with us throughout the Reformation and the
European Enlightenment, both of which have influenced western
scholars, who have reflected the notion of being the 'upper ones'.
This has filtered into western theology, which assumes an air of superiority over the work of biblical scholars in the Global South and sees
itself as the most pristine source of knowledge; its reliability is seen
as second only to the Bible itself. The western mission enterprise has
faithfully exported this theology around the world, where it apparently has everything to teach but little to learn. What western scholars still do not seem to realize is that this assumption comes from a
deeply ingrained and culture-bound understanding of the Bible and,
in my view, contributes to the crisis in western evangelicalism. British
researcher Eddie Arthur concurs in his analysis of the situation:

> Western Christianity exists in a culture where the notion of the supernat-
> ural has been broadly rejected in favour of scientific rationalism. If you
> can't see it or count it, it doesn't exist. In this atmosphere, Christian belief

in a supernatural, interventionist God has been eroded . . . For the most part, Africans [and other people in the Global South] don't live in this post-enlightenment spiritual vacuum. Their world is rich with spirits and angels who have an impact on the lives of men and women.[7]

An example of this was the Indian Bible scholar who told me that when he gives papers at a western theological symposium, he finds that papers from western scholars are referred to as 'theology', while a paper from the Global South is referred to publicly as 'an Asian perspective'. A board member of one of the organizations I worked with would agree about the existence of a theological periphery and even referred to the non-*English* members of the board as 'the Celtic fringe'. Such attitudes appear to be rooted in Christendom and are tantamount to 'theological imperialism'.

It is important to remember that Jesus did not speak English and there are probably no white people in the Bible. If the biblical writers were living in the West today, they too would be identified as part of the 'ethnic minority'.

Global Hegemony

Hegemony embeds itself in a culture, a nation state, a police force, an army, a religion, or in commercial expansion. We see it exhibited in China's economic expansion in the West, its treatment of the Uyghur people, its military repression of Tibet, and its control in Taiwan and Hong Kong. It is also clear in Russia's interference in Ukraine and the former Soviet states. The economic form of hegemony operates *in* and *from* Saudi Arabia as that country's oil-wealth is used to drive Islamic propagation via mosque building and the funding of Islamic propagators, such as Zakir Naik who received a $200,000 award from the Saudi government,[8] and via funds discreetly supplied to jihadi fighters in a bid to achieve a Wahhabi-inspired religious empire across the Middle East; the methods used include waging proxy wars in Syria, Yemen and Afghanistan, as well as encouraging terrorist intimidation in places such as India, Kashmir, Sri Lanka, the Horn of Africa and Nigeria.[9]

Social Hegemony

During the Covid-19 pandemic of 2020–21, British Muslim communities on the ground were largely ignored by the UK government when a volunteer taskforce was set up by Muslims to work with government agencies to promote the official messaging. By the time the government realized it needed the local knowledge, it was too late – new spikes of infection had begun in South Asian communities in the north of England, and many blamed the South Asian community for causing them. This suggests a government default position to interact paternalistically with those deemed to be deprived sections of society.

Only those who have grown up on the wrong side of hegemony can appreciate the polite social exclusion of those who are not really considered one of the 'upper ones'. An Indian friend of mine is a successful businessman and said to me: 'At times, my school tie is not quite right.' The 'old school tie' is a quintessentially English phenomenon, going back to the days when senior politicians, professionals and masters of industry all went to the same cluster of schools and universities, creating a set of alumni whose members formed an elite layer in a hierarchical society. Although the practice of excluding those who do not share the same 'school tie' has reduced, it has not entirely disappeared and is still going on, dictated by gender, social class, education, ethnicity and even accent.

Just Deal with It . . .

The way to navigate our way around Mount Hegemony is to understand how hegemony shapes the way our nation understands its place in the world. We must then accept that, within a society that is hegemonic, the chips are stacked in the favour of those whose face 'fits'. A key factor in this is the part played by race in the pecking order, so this is our segue to the next chapter.

If hegemony is a *root* of racial superiority, racism is its *fruit*. The two are strongly interrelated but need teasing out, which we will do as we analyse Mount Ethnos. What is racism? Where does it come from? Is there such a thing as 'institutional' racism? How do we navigate it in our interaction with a Muslim? Let us see.

5

Mount Ethnos

Racism as part of human nature and the impacts on church, state, and faith organizations

> The problem of the century is the problem of the colour-line.
>
> William Edward Burghardt Du Bois[1]

In this chapter we see how racism comes from hegemony, which has links to imperialism. We identify where racism comes from and define and describe the difference between 'personal' and 'systemic' racism. We also recognize that a significant number of Muslims in the West are from African and West Indian families. We indicate how colonial roots and slavery affect the psyche of many Muslims today, blocking healthy interaction.

If imperialism (chapter 3) carries within it the notion of hegemony (chapter 4), we also find that hegemony carries within it the notion of the *supremacy* behind the racial pecking order that is racism. This is the next mountain blockage to interaction between non-Muslims and Muslims. Racism is a complex and multifaceted issue, so I will take two steps back and come at it from the angle that I think works better for people of colour.

A Messianic Jew once said to me: 'Christianity is "Judaism for export".' When I asked her what she meant, she pointed out that the Great Commission of Christ is to 'Go and make disciples of all *nations*' (Matt. 28:19) (i.e. people of non-Jewish ethnicity). In the original Greek, the word for 'nations' is *ethne* (ἔθνη), from which we get the English word 'ethnic'. *Ethne* does not mean a nation state as we would understand it but a racial subgroup within a political nation state. That conversation was significant, coming as it did from a Messianic Jew whose cultural background taught her that God is the sole preserve of the Jew. Yet a growing number of ethnic Jews are changing their allegiance to Jesus Christ and understand that Christ sends them to every ethnic group on the planet. Jewish believers in Jesus seem to understand that they are not sent to Gentiles *in spite* of them being racially different from Jews but *because* of it. The Great Commission of Christ is pan-racial in its inclusivity. From this angle, we get a better grasp of the fact that racism, in all its subtlety, is a significant blockage to the completion of the Great Commission.

What Is Racism?

The definition of 'racism' gets skewed by subjectivity in us all. For example, when determined solely by the lived experience of people of colour, it inevitably carries a wound in their soul, to this day. Nor can it be determined solely through the lens of white people for fear that the concept itself becomes subconsciously manipulated by hegemony (i.e. the 'upper ones' writing history). When we legislate against *personal* acts of racism, it sends racism underground, where it festers, which is arguably worse. The word 'racism' can be narrowed down by dictionary definitions as follows:

> Racism is the internal belief (often subconscious) that, based on people's physical appearance, we can determine what behaviour can be expected in terms of culture, social patterns or religion, the assumption being that one race is, in some way, superior to another. Such a belief tends to lead to external reactions such as prejudice, discrimination or overt antagonism against people of a different race or ethnicity.[2]

Tariq Modood is helpful when he describes racism as the act of 'including all members of an ethnic group as falling under the same negative expectations, based on their cultural or religious practices, and then [to] vilify, marginalize, discriminate, or treat them as second-class citizens'.[3] This shows that 'racism' is a portmanteau word because it has at least two aspects: internal invisible attitudes and external visible actions. An academic debate is ongoing about how racism takes root within a society. Does it start internally in the mind of an individual and then express itself in external behaviour, or does it start in the external structures of a society and work its way into the individual mind?

The difference between the Bible and the newly trending 'Critical Race Theory' (which blames racism on white people) is that, according to the Bible, people of *all* ethnicities are carriers of the racism virus. It seems to be an endemic aspect of human nature like a pandemic awaiting a vaccine. The symptoms manifest in three distinct ways from expression within a group to expression in an individual (i.e. from the macro level to the micro):

- *institutional racism* – systems which disadvantage and disenfranchise people based on ethnicity
- *group racism* – policies or non-verbal herd instincts that exist in an organization, a social institution, a government department, and so on
- *personal racism* – an internal belief, attitude or expectation based on people's ethnicity.

Racism as Human Nature

Feeling that we are better than other people is not the sole preserve of white people. To place ourselves higher in a notional pecking order seems to help all ethnicities to feel better about themselves. This plays out in the caste system in India, the anti-Semitism of Nazi

Germany, the neo-Nazi thinking of racist groups today, the African tribal conflicts in Rwanda (Tutsi versus Hutu)[4] and Nigeria (Jukun versus Tive),[5] or the racial superiority of the Fulani tribe – the largest and most widely spread in West Africa. The same pattern is found in Saudi Arabia, which effectively colonized Egypt, North Africa and Sudan and still harbours a superior attitude to these nations. The story also plays out for the swarthy Rohingya, who are subjugated by the pale-skinned Burmese in Myanmar.

When I lived among the light-skinned urban people of northern Egypt, I found that they look down on the black (Nilotic) rural Egyptians of the far south. The preference for fairer skin-tone in the Middle East is likely to be rooted in the fact that the Arabs were prolific slave traders. The Arabic word for slave is *'abd*. As a result, in Arab culture, the words 'black' and 'slave' became psychologically synonymous even though the actual word for black is *iswid*.

I am of Caribbean descent and so grew up with the awareness that the West Indian 'large islanders' would look down on the 'small islanders'. We could go on, but suffice it to say here that the same pattern is found among the English who tend to look down on the Irish, white northern urbanized Americans who look down on their white counterparts in the rural southern states, Canadians who look down on the wilderness people of Newfoundland (i.e. the Newfie), Pakistanis who look down on Bangladeshis . . . Even the Muslim Council of Britain (MCB) has recognized that South Asian and Arab Muslims are prone to look down on black Muslims.[6]

The Ethnicities of British Muslims

As a 'visible minority', Muslims become targets of racism, whether it be polite or abusive. The majority of British Muslims are South Asian (i.e. Pakistani, Bangladeshi, Afghani and Gujarati Indian), with other ethnicities hailing from the Middle East, North Africa, Iran, sub-Saharan Africa, and South East Asia (e.g. Malays and Indonesians).

However, a lesser-known ethnic group is the West Indians who are converting to Islam. Researcher Richard Reddie found that 9% of British West Indians identify as Muslim[7] and tend to come from families that are either dysfunctional[8] or keen churchgoers.[9] These converts perceive Islam to be a confident and counter-cultural community that can deliver the aspirations of the Rastafarian movement that was popular in the 1970s and 1980s. The felt need of these converts is said to be *identity* and a doctrine that is 'combative and prepared to confront Western hypocrisy head-on in the name of truth'.[10]

I believe that, like Rastafarianism, the conversion trend to Islam will also pass; I say this because this sort of allegiance is a sociopolitical phenomenon rather than a 'spiritual' one. I am informed anecdotally that the average convert lasts for about five years. Imam Talib Abdur-Rashid is the leader of the black Muslims in New York and describes black converts to Islam as a brotherhood who 'arrived in different ships' but 'all being in the same boat'.[11] This is true on both sides of the Atlantic among African Muslims and Caribbean Muslim converts. The different ships were either a slave ship or a passenger liner; the one was voluntary immigration, and the other was forced.

It seems to me that perhaps the foundational reason behind the Caribbean conversion phenomenon is the damage done through past white colonialism and hegemony (chapters 3, 4). This gets perpetuated in well-intentioned patronization of black people as a way of assuaging the sense of post-colonial guilt, which we will meet again when we discuss political correctness (chapter 6), and again when we discuss the marginalization and even the strident abuse that can be experienced by people of colour (chapter 7).

My heart is deeply saddened by what I am told by black people who give up on 'white churches'. Those congregations manage to be free of much of the colonial mental baggage, only to fail people of colour by meticulous adherence to their denominational expectations. This causes a lack of imagination in church leaders, who do not seem to attempt to grasp the issues and the urgent need for greater racial and cultural inclusivity in church life – whether the congregations be white, middle class or black-led. A whole book could be written about churches which appear to be stuck in non-negotiable routines of worship, culturally blinkered theology, and anaemic forms of spirituality – which often fail to nourish the Anglo-Saxon soul, let alone those of other social background, race or culture. Consequently, many British churches are self-referencing but disconnected from the issues of our day.

Black Muslims

No one is going to sense this disconnect like black people, which is why Imam Talib says that to be black and Muslim is to be 'twice black'. There is a double stigma that is both racial and religious because, as a visible minority, people see:

- someone's colour and social class
- the fact that some choose Islam after a Christian upbringing
- a 'home-grown' convert, which is also a political statement as well as a security threat
- the scary potential that a black convert may become radicalized.

Race Is Not Faith

We have already said that it is a disservice to a Muslim to conflate their race with their religion, as though they are inextricable. If they were, people like me might well have chosen to be a Muslim, rather than a believer in Jesus Christ. The only people for whom race and faith are essentially the same thing are Jews, whether they practise Judaism or not. The same cannot be said of a Muslim because their race may be rooted anywhere from Mauritania to Indonesia, where there are also compatriots who are Christian, Buddhist, Hindu or Sikh. Their family embraced Islam due to history, politics and social expectation, rather than being merely a *racial* consideration.

In Arabic, the word *muslim* behaves like an adjective rather than a noun. It describes someone who is a certain way (i.e. they have a lifestyle submitted to God as an adherent of Islam). Therefore, being Muslim is something you *do*, not something you *are*. The correct grammar is not 'She is *a* Muslim' as we have it in English, but rather 'She *is* Muslim' (i.e. it is *how* she lives). Unfortunately, in the West, dictionary definitions tend to corroborate the politically correct notion that all Muslims are religious, and that race and religion are the same thing. This encourages people to hold expectations about someone's culture, social patterns and religious practice based on their ethnicity. This may be well-meaning, but it makes the judgement based on a racial distinction, which is, technically speaking, racist. Most Muslims are aware of this distinction and are often proud of their ethnicity as being separate from their Islam. We should not rob them of this by lumping all Muslims together as an amorphous mass and then getting jittery about the mass we have created in our own mind, which is Islamophobia.

Will the Real Islamophobia Please Stand Up?

The term 'Islamophobia' means 'a fear of Islam' and was first coined around 1920 by academic Alain Quellien.[12] It has come into popular use in more recent years only as the social issues surrounding the Muslim presence in the West have come to the fore politically. It is sad that in the current PC climate (see chapter 6) people can be attacked by the liberal left for trying to separate out race and religion. If we did so more often, the behaviour of people in any faith group could rightly be called out where necessary. So why has the use of the word 'Islamophobia' come about?

A governmental All-Party Parliamentary Group (APPG) produced a report that tries to define the term 'Islamophobia'. It concluded that it is 'rooted in racism' and that 'it is a type of racism that targets expressions of Muslimness or perceived Muslimness'.[13] This too is a well-meant statement which has an element of truth in it. However, it is flawed in that it conflates 'race', 'culture' and 'religion' as one,[14] which makes anything that impinges on these a shorthand for 'racism' and/or 'Islamophobia'; this was the problem for which Trevor Phillips was castigated, as we saw in chapter 1.

Another complaint about the definition was that it puts too much 'out of bounds', which potentially shuts down discussion about controversial issues that are arguably *cultural* in some Islamic states but not required in Islam; for example, female genital mutilation (FMG) in the Horn of Africa, parts of Sudan and elsewhere, or the violent exorcism of alleged evil spirits from children in parts of West Africa among Muslims *and Christians*. It is naive to assume that, just because something is cultural (or indeed religious), it is right, healthy or acceptable. If that were the case, we could cite the issue of binding girls' feet in China, or the lengthening of girls' necks in Thailand, or the burning of Indian widows on the funeral pyre of their deceased husbands (*sati*). All this would still be going on today if it had not been challenged as a violation of human rights. In a similar way, the clumsy concept of 'Islamophobia' does not always help Muslims or non-Muslims; in fact, it has often made things worse.

The 'fear' in Islamophobia is not necessarily of Islam per se (though some may have that); nor is it necessarily a fear of *all* Muslims (that would surely be 'Muslophobia'); nor indeed is it a fear of someone's ethnicity (though that can come into it). Rather, it seems to me that the *fear* is of the totalitarian attitudes and terrorist violence of the Muslims on the lunatic fringe of Islam; a fear shared by many Muslims.

If we were afraid of, or wanted to challenge the behaviour of, the Irish Republican Army (IRA), no one would accuse us of 'Catholophobia' or even 'Christophobia' (i.e. a fear of Christianity), yet when we are afraid of Muslim extremism, or challenge the bullying behaviour of the minority of assertive and political Muslims, we may well be accused of 'Islamophobia'; this does not seem logical.

Racism in the Bible

We have said that racism is a virus that is endemic in fallen human nature. Ethnicity is therefore a theme found in the Bible. For example, when Moses married a Cushite woman (i.e. Sudanese) it provoked a racist reaction from Miriam and Aaron, who criticized Moses publicly. The incident incurred divine displeasure on Moses' behalf (Num. 12:1ff.).

A New Testament example was the long-standing bad attitude of Jews towards Samaritans (John 4:9), which had acrimonious roots in 2 Kings 17:24–34, and resurfaced with Sanballet the Samaritan who was anti-Semitic (Neh. 2:19). It surfaced again in the attitude of the apostle Peter to all non-Jews. However, when Peter was faced with his racism, he did a U-turn and said: 'how true it is that God does not show favouritism but accepts from every nation the one who fears him and does what is right' (Acts 10:34–35).

The apostle Paul voiced the saying: 'Cretans are *always* liars, evil brutes, lazy gluttons' (Titus 1:12). He was quoting the Greek philosopher Epimenides, who was himself from Crete and was castigating his own people. However, the sentiment is a classic example of racial stereotyping.

According to the vision of St John the Divine in the book of Revelation, the culmination of the ages includes the abolition of racism, when *every* 'nation', 'tribe', 'race' (*ethne*) and 'language' is included in the kingdom of God (see Rev. 7:9). They are *all* affirmed as included and there is a celebration of the multi-ethnic church, which becomes an icon of the triumph of redemption as the Great Commission of Christ ends. That is then, but we are living now as witnesses to the turbulence, as racial harmony struggles to find its level in society; but why is this?

Reverse Racism

Racism persists partly because the issue of race is like a political football that people kick back and forth to gain advantage over one another. At the time of writing, the football is changing direction and we are on the cusp of an era of 'reverse racism', where strident black people are placing blame on *all* white people for past acts of white supremacy such as the slave trade, segregation laws, and then the lingering racial prejudice and social disadvantage. This resentment erupted after 25 May 2020 in response to the apparently wilful killing of George Floyd by a white police officer. Floyd was a black American who was a convicted felon accused of resisting arrest. The police officer knelt on Floyd's neck on and off for over eight minutes, restricting his windpipe and ignoring his pleading: 'I can't breathe!'[15] This murder strengthened the view that the Ku Klux Klan simply exchanged their white robes for police uniforms.

In the mayhem that followed, the Black Lives Matter (BLM) protesters (black and white) were infiltrated by factions driven by 'cultural Marxism', which is the application of Marxist principles of egalitarianism not just to financial arrangements but to abolish racism and the oppression of sexual minorities. Such groups seem unaware that such injustice is rife in traditionally Marxist states, such as Russia; yet they remain committed to subversion of the status quo in the West. Anarchist groups such as Antifa are simply the better-known extreme of the covert networks, which operate under the radar wherever there is opportunity for civil disturbance, regardless of the original trigger for a protest.

People are becoming concerned about this herd mentality, which is enticing protesters to naively jump onboard anything that may appear to be a 'just' cause, while being oblivious to the fact that strings are often being pulled by questionable groups with a sinister agenda. Why is this mindset developing?

Professor Carol Swain is a black observer who identifies a lack of teaching on critical thinking in western schools and universities. She bases this on evidence of the infiltration of Marxists into the BLM leadership and among their followers. These individuals, she says, are using race to pursue a Marxist agenda.[16] The British franchise of BLM is also thought to be run by an inner circle of fewer than a dozen people who intend to remain anonymous. On Facebook and the crowd-funding page GoFundMe (which netted them a million pounds), the leaders of BLM may even be majority white, but they insist they are committed to dismantling imperialism, capitalism, white supremacy, patriarchy, homophobia and lesbophobia, and are for the abolition of the police, prisons, the stigmatization of HIV, the reversal of climate change, the emancipation of the Gaza Strip, and the toppling of the Israeli government.[17]

The George Floyd murder is a gift to such people, because it sparked unrest worldwide. In Bristol in the UK, black and white protesters lost patience after lobbying the local authority to remove a statue of the slave trader Edward Colston, who was also a major philanthropist in the city. Like others, he used the docks to amass his fortune by slave trafficking. The current mayor of Bristol, Marvin Rees, is of Caribbean heritage and made the point that Germany has no statues or roads named after Adolf Hitler, so why should the UK honour known slave traders? These men should be consigned to museums as a warning, rather than being commemorated in an age that has long abandoned the practice.[18]

If racism is endemic to human nature, as we have seen above, why does the USA get profiled in such a poor light?

Why American Racism Is So Iconic

The popular impression is that *only* the United States has engaged in slavery and struggles with race issues to this day. This is a false impression, but there are understandable reasons why it exists. Let us take a step back to say that history shows that slavery, and racism of all kinds, has always been a global phenomenon. For example, the Greek and Roman empires were built and maintained by enslaved peoples, and several Arab nations were slavers from the ninth century AD.

Unlike the black community in the USA, the influx of slaves in the Persian Gulf included various ethnicities, including black people; but black males were castrated, or 'made eunuchs' in biblical language: 'There are eunuchs who were born that way, and there are eunuchs who have been made eunuchs by others [slaves] – and there are those who choose to live like eunuchs for the sake of the kingdom of heaven' (Matt. 19:12). The Ethiopian eunuch who met the apostle Philip was probably made so by an African royal household (Acts 8:26–39).

In the modern Gulf, the darker-skinned Arabs we see are the mixed-race descendants of Arab men and their enslaved African women. Spain, Portugal, France and Britain were also slaver nations, so although its record has not been good, the USA is *not* alone in this.

There are also examples beyond the issue of slavery. Take, for instance, the founding of Australia when the British used state-sanctioned racism to enter sparsely populated Aboriginal land and declare it 'empty', or *terra nullius* (Latin for 'nobody's land'). The British chose *not* to notice the Aboriginal people who stood and watched Captain Cook's ships arrive and who later died, at the hands of the British, trying to protect their land. These 'first nation' people were effectively declared 'non-existent'. Within living memory, we have seen the practice of taking Aboriginal children away from their families to have the 'blackness' bred out of them as a way of assimilation into the white population. This sad legacy has continued as a controversial national blind spot in Australian society. The makers of a recent documentary found that, while there are some positive signs that change is slowly coming, there are still examples of overt racism in Australia today.[19]

The documentary followed the career of the Aussie Rules football star Adam Goodes, who is of Aboriginal descent. Goodes suffered racial abuse on the pitch and from management, and when he stood his ground and called out racism he was vilified on social media as being sensitive. Goodes became a broken man, which ultimately ended his illustrious career prematurely. His experience eventually earned him national recognition as the campaigner who has done most to challenge and change the unconscious bias of racism in Australia.

America's Journey with Race

The sort of evidence presented above underlines why the USA has its unfair reputation on race. The likely reasons include the fact that all three strands of racism – personal, group and institutional – have occurred in relatively recent decades; however, the challenge comes because America's successes and failures in addressing them have happened in the context of protest movements led by some high-profile civil rights champions, and in the glare of the media spotlight. This has kept the race issue alive, which has benefited people of colour on both sides of the Atlantic on a journey through three distinct periods, as follows.

The slave era (1501–1865)

Britain abolished slavery in 1833 and the USA did so in 1865, while Saudi Arabia continued until 1960 and Mauritania until 1981; both stopped under international pressure, but researchers claim the slave trade still goes on covertly in Arab countries. John Azumah points out that over the past few decades, the West has been browbeaten by political correctness to admit the evils of the slave trade by 'Christian' European nations, while retaining the idealized notion that the glory days of the Islamic Empire did *not* involve slavery. The reality is that Muslims were doing it too, and on an industrial scale.[20]

The segregation era (1865–1964)

The next part of the American (and British) journey includes the lingering segregation that followed the abolition of slavery. It should be said that although the experience of segregation in the USA and the UK differs in *degree*, it had the same *kind* of impact on black people. The scenes of a segregated America show draconian laws in force, separating blacks and whites in public spaces; while in post-war Britain, immigrants of colour were invited by the government to come in and help rebuild the economy, but they were rejected by the public.

The era of remedial action (1965 onwards)

It seems the missing piece of the jigsaw has always been the need for a more radical investment in social development through government partnering *with* black communities to assist them in developing the tools for 'self-help'. However, this is not how it went. The respected black American academic Thomas Sowell points out that, instead of a much-needed levelling-up process (particularly in the USA), short-term social welfare handouts were given. This may have been well-intentioned, but it threw good money after bad because it fostered a culture of dependency, poor housing, ghettos, fewer educational opportunities, higher levels of unemployment, dysfunctional families, widespread drug use, soaring crime rates and a greater black presence in prisons.[21] All this has brought a higher bill than if the causes of the problem had been addressed once and for all in the first place.

In this sense, it is likely that every multiracial society has a story of racial inequality and racial prejudice to tell; it is just that America gets unfairly singled out. Thomas Sowell goes on to call out 'positive discrimination' as being as bad as slavery because it is an unintended consequence of 'welfare dependency', which has done the greater damage by facilitating a regression into barbarism where black neighbourhoods are preyed upon by black hoodlums.[22] Most black people are socially excluded in some way and left with a simmering resentment over being allowed to slip through the cracks – hence their sense of victimhood and resentment leading to 'reverse racism' against white people.

It must also be said here that there is a significant minority of black people who do manage to navigate their way through the system into senior positions in *all* walks of life, including Barack Obama, the first US president of colour, and Vice President Kamala Harris, who has a dual ethnic heritage: a Jamaican father and Indian mother. This spread of representation is something the UK has still not achieved, at least not to the same extent and prominence, in areas such as the armed forces, the police, the judiciary, the football industry and academia. The proverbial 'glass ceiling' remains for people of colour.

On a more positive note, the British police service is now taking steps to become more ethnically inclusive due to the fact that in 2019 there were only 15 non-white dog handlers out of 734, and 2 non-white mounted police officers out of 184. It is thought that selection processes have been affected by unconscious bias and possible cronyism.[23]

The point here is that nations that have experienced all three strands of racism – *personal, group* and *institutional* – are still in the process of screening it out of their system; it takes time. In this sense, British racism is a classic and longer-standing case. For example, racism was clearly *institutionalized* at government level during the slave trade. It was *group* in the civil service during the days of empire when the highest award given for overseas colonial service was the Order of St Michael and St George. At the centre of the decoration was a picture of St Michael, who is white, standing with a foot on the neck of the devil, who is depicted as a black man; the murder of George Floyd was an echo of this scene. Sir David Attenborough was recently made a knight of this order but, due to complaints about this imagery, the graphic has been updated to reflect the devil as someone of nondescript ethnicity.

Racism was also rife at the *personal* level in post-war Britain, when in public opinion there was an unofficial 'colour bar', and boarding-house owners openly displayed signs in their windows saying things such as: 'Blacks, Pakistanis, Irish and dogs not wanted'. The colour bar may be officially over, but it continues to fly under the radar. Anecdotal evidence is occasionally obtained, for instance when investigative journalists apply for jobs using bogus Muslim or black-sounding names. When they compare the responses to their applications with those who have a traditional white name, the racial prejudice is revealed.

All three of these levels continue, in different ways, to contribute to the ongoing slowness in the social levelling up of people of colour, which allows ethnicity to become a glass ceiling.

I Have Some Concerns

Things are moving slowly in the right direction. However, in light of the above, I have four concerns about the current state of the 'race debate', as follows.

First, the debate needs to be not just about what happened in the past, but about what happens now and where we need to get to in the future. I say this because, on the one hand, the slave era is long over, so it is a stretch for any black person today to automatically assume the moral high ground, from which to pontificate about 'punishing' the descendants of white slave-traders, as though slavery is their fault. On the other hand, no white person is morally obligated to placate the descendants of the victims of slavery by imposing 'positive discrimination' (affirmative action). While well-meant, this too is – technically speaking – a *racist* response if we go by the dictionary definition of racism.

Second, the issue we face today is not one of 'race' per se but of the social disparity it has left behind, which perpetuates racist stereotyping, which in turn perpetuates ongoing prejudicial behaviour. Surely the issue at stake in the twenty-first century is one of *social justice*, which returns self-worth and dignity to people of colour and addresses the reasons why some get on the wrong side of the law. This sort of response to racial justice is overdue and, in my view, is a moral responsibility for politicians.

Third, the 'tit for tat' of reverse racism has never worked. It was espoused by black rights campaigners such as Wallace Fard Muhammad, the founder of the Nation of Islam in the 1930s with Malcolm X as its spokesperson, and also by Huey P. Newton as a spokesperson for the revolutionary Black Panther Party in the 1960s. If Black Lives Matter (the organization) takes the route of reprisal, it is also setting itself up to fail.

Fourth, while the sentiment and 'cause' of Black Lives Matter is laudable, the evidence suggests that racism (i.e. 'A') gets confused with the social deprivation it can cause (i.e. 'B'). The two are inextricably linked, and it seems intuitive to assume that solving 'A' will automatically solve 'B'. However, in my view, this is too simplistic because it is more likely that solving 'B' will resolve 'A'. I say this because it is the impacts of racism that do most damage and cause black people to give up and sink into bitterness and anger, which is why 95% of black murders are black on black, and why black Americans, who form only 13% of the US population, in 2018 were responsible for 90% of 'interracial violent victimization' (race-based abuse); and in 2019 black Americans were responsible for 50% of hate crimes against Jews and gay people.[24] This is why the *fruit* of racism is more toxic than racism itself.

Black Approaches to Civil Rights

Campaigning for issues of social justice via passive resistance is harder and takes longer, but it has been championed by people such as Martin Luther King Jr, who operated like Gandhi. The aggressive approach was championed by black Muslim individuals and groups, such as Malcolm X, the Black Panthers and the Nation of Islam. Such movements managed to bring to the world's attention the 450 years of damage done to the black psyche, but they were less effective in achieving what is needed to repair the damage. As a result, even though laws were changed, both the USA and UK continue to struggle with overhauling the social arrangements that perpetuate racial prejudice, so that the negative impacts can heal.

As both an active Christian and a person of colour, I have experienced the personal damage done by racism, but I believe the solution starts with *recognition* of the damage done, which is not the same as *blame*. The solution does not lie in 'revenge' for the past, nor necessarily 'reparations' in the present. We have seen that the problem has proved to be deeper than government handouts. Nor should we (black and white) give in to a culture of 'victimhood' or 'guilt'. Those who take up the worthy cause of 'levelling up' today face the same fork in the road as the earlier civil rights campaigners: will the goal be achieved by constructive or destructive means? I fully understand and have sympathy with the Black Lives Matter 'cause' and can even understand 'taking the knee'; however, it bothers me to see people raise a clenched fist in the salute of the former aggressive Black Power Movement.

That said, I reserve my biggest support for the growing number of black people who are identifying with the lesser-known cause of

'Blacks *against* Black Lives Matter'. This movement stands against the militant element in BLM and calls for more concrete action to help black communities to empower themselves to climb out of the social hole created by the aftermath of slavery and segregation.

We need black leaders today who will model the moral authority of the likes of Lord Wilberforce, who spearheaded the abolition of slavery in Britain, or Martin Luther King Jr and James Baldwin (peaceful black civil rights champions in the USA), or Nelson Mandela, who became the figurehead in the abolition of apartheid in South Africa. Although these people were imperfect, they left a legacy of change, not by tearing things down or smashing up property or injuring people (or worse), but by modelling something better.

It is a Christly instinct to see social justice as a moral imperative which, as a universal principle, is incumbent not only on Christ-followers but also on people of all faiths and none. This is a cause in which we need one another, but is it true that *institutional* racism is still a thing today?

How Real Is Institutional Racism?

The term 'institutional racism' attempts to describe the deeply imbedded inequalities in a society that cause ethnic minorities to become vulnerable due to social inequalities.

In a debate at the Oxford Union, 'institutional racism' was defined as treating ethnic minorities prejudicially; for example, in the USA, black people get a lower credit-score, struggle to get a loan to buy a house, live in poorer neighbourhoods and have less access to state funding for education.[25] With such poor prospects, young black Americans drift into crime and come up against the criminal justice system. If they possess 28 grams of cocaine, they get a five-year prison sentence, compared with white people who need to possess 50 grams of cocaine to get the same term. After prison, black people are denied parole more often than white people, spend longer on probation, remain a felon for longer, are unable to get housing benefit, cannot get loans, or vote, or travel abroad, and find it harder to get employment.

The black American analyst David Webb limits his use of the word 'institutional' to situations where there is an intentional 'social contract' or codified law, such as nations which sanctioned the slave trade, the supremacy of the Aryan race in Nazi Germany, South Africa's apartheid regime, or China and its treatment of the Uyghur people.[26] I would agree with Webb because I too prefer to use the term 'systemic' (or structural) racism, which helps account for the less obvious forms of racism. Analyst Gene Joo refers to this subtler form as racism having 'retreated into the shadows of our collective consciousness, waging a perpetual guerilla war against justice and equality'.[27]

The black American analyst Coleman Hughes says the more recent West Indian immigrants to the USA tend, on all social indicators, to do much better than indigenous 'African Americans' whose families have been resident since the slave era, because the West Indians are culturally and historically distinct.[28] Indigenous black Americans were *involuntary* arrivals who were repressed and, after emancipation, have struggled to compete, while West Indian Americans (including members of my own family) migrated voluntarily and have a drive to work hard and achieve their goals, sometimes even outperforming their white American counterparts.

Black American TV host Larry Elder is one analyst who uses the term 'Black American' but rejects the term 'African American', saying it is meaningless unless we talk about 'White Americans' too.[29] Black Americans may not have been in the USA for as long as 'Native Americans' but they are as *American* as the early white immigrants. Elder also challenges the media-driven perception of so-called 'racial killings'. For example, in Baltimore a black man, Freddie Grey, died in a police incident, yet Baltimore is 45% black, the majority of the city council are black, the two senior police officials were black, the mayor was black, yet it was called a 'racist' killing by the press. The media also downplay the fact that in the USA more black people are shot dead than any other group, and the majority of these deaths are a result of black people shooting other black people. This brings us back to the issue of social injustice and serious inequality.

Perhaps the best way to identify 'systemic racism' is by looking at the facts about its characteristics. For example, according to the *Race Disparity Audit* (revised 2018), 9% of black people in the UK are unemployed compared to 4% of the white population.[30] On every social indicator, black and Asian people in the UK score poorly compared to their white counterparts. Karamat Iqbal has researched in detail how the British education system has disenfranchised Pakistani boys in Birmingham.[31]

Racism in Public Life

Charges of systemic racism (i.e. institutional or structural) have been levelled against organizations such as the London Metropolitan Police ('the Met') over their use of 'stop and search' powers,[32] and also their handling of racially motivated crime, such as the murder of an 18-year-old black youth, Stephen Lawrence, in 1993 by a gang of white racist youths as he waited at a bus stop in Eltham, south-east London. It happened again over the Met's apparent systematic resistance to the promotion of non-white officers.[33] The same is thought to be true in areas such as the civil and diplomatic services. When racism becomes systemic it creates a 'glass ceiling' effect, which is invisible until the wrong people try to pass through it.

The Queen led the way by giving royal assent to the marriage of Prince Harry to Meghan Markle. There was genuine rejoicing in Britain over the wedding, and the Queen soon included Meghan in high-profile royal duties, embracing Archie as a great-grandchild. This indicated an end to the historic bias towards white-only European diversity in the British royal family. Negative press started as Harry and Meghan championed action against climate change while flying around in private jets. Reports followed of friction with staff, before the one-sided interview with Oprah Winfrey that was heavy on insinuation and light on detail. Fact checkers soon found holes in many of the claims being made, giving rise to suspicions about Harry and Meghan's 'woke' motives. As a person of colour, I feel Meghan did not think the opportunity she faced to bring colour into the royal establishment was good enough as her life's work. Instead, it seems her demeanour prompted the friction, which was 'spun' as a reaction to her colour. This seems neither wholly true nor fair. In contrast to Meghan's approach, there is Emma Thynn,[34] who sustained overt racism in the British aristocracy, but soldiered on through it. She is the daughter of a white English socialite mother and a Nigerian oil baron. As such, Emma had an elite upbringing in the upper echelons of British society; however, when she met and married Ceawlin, Viscount Weymouth (making her the first mixed-race viscountess Weymouth), she was told the marriage would 'ruin a four-hundred-year-old Anglo-Saxon bloodline'. Her mother-in-law, Lady Bath, refused to attend the wedding and even to meet her subsequent grandchildren.

A similar reaction awaited the Nigerian writer Dillibe Onyeama, who was the first black student at the prestigious Eton College. He graduated in 1969 after being taunted daily by fellow students who would ask: 'Why are you black?', 'How many maggots are there in your hair?' and 'Does your mother wear a bone in her nose?' When he excelled academically, he was accused of cheating and has recently published a book about the racial climate at that time.[35]

Racism in Church Denominations

The Church of England has found that only 1.2% of its clergy are from an ethnic minority background,[36] and on 11 February 2020 the following apology appeared on its website:

> Members [of the General Synod] unanimously backed a motion to 'lament' and apologise for conscious and unconscious racism encountered by 'countless' black, Asian and minority ethnic (BAME) Anglicans arriving in Britain from 1948 and in subsequent years, when seeking to find a home in the Church of England. Synod expressed 'gratitude to God'

for the 'indispensable' contribution to the mission, ministry, prayer and worship of the Church of England made by people of BAME descent. Members voted to redouble efforts to combat racism and to work towards greater participation of BAME Anglicans in all areas of Church life.[37]

Yet that same month, a black trainee vicar, Augustine Tanner-Ihm, was refused a placement in a 'monochrome' parish on the grounds that it was felt he would not be 'comfortable'. When this became known, the Diocese of St Albans issued an apology for the 'poor choice of words' (but *not* for the rejection itself).[38]

As a boy, in the 1960s, I was accepted as possibly the first black head chorister in a traditional Anglican church, St Mary the Virgin, a civic and university church in the centre of my native city Nottingham. When I trained as a teacher, in the 1970s, I was urged to become the first black head teacher in Britain. I was also probably the first non-white mission director in the UK in the 1990s. I reminisce because, during the past decade, things have been returning to more overt forms of racism online. 'Right-wing' groups have provoked clashes and forced Muslims to be seen not as 'strangers in the midst' but as 'the enemy within', even though many were British born.

Racism in Christian Organizations

There are around 240 member agencies in the Global Connections mission network in Britain, yet for reasons outside its control, as far as I am aware, there are only about four non-white CEOs. In local churches, racist sentiments are extremely covert, but I remember an occasion when I was preaching in a church in the north of England and the minister was brave enough to tell me that the congregation was not comfortable seeing a black face in the pulpit. Racism can and does exist among active Christians, who learn how to bypass employment law by the careful use of language.

After three decades I have learned to spot the signs, such as the number of non-white trustees on an organization's board or among senior staff. In the case of cross-cultural mission organizations, the question is: how many staff have roots in the geographical area or cultures of the agency's work?

Among the personal complaints I have received are accounts from West Indian and South Asian women and men who have told me about their struggles in the ranks of western Christian organizations. One Indian shared how he had felt constantly pressured to think and behave like a middle-class white person, before being manoeuvred out of the agency as a 'poor fit'. Agencies with this kind of issue tend to be those founded in the colonial era, which inculcate a blind spot over race and gender.

It is true that if we think something is there, we are more likely to look for it; however, logic also dictates that if we assume something is *not* there (or should not be there), we are less likely to look for it, let alone find it! When racism does exist in Christian circles, it is rarely challenged formally by those who suffer it, because to challenge something is not seen as the *Christian* thing to do – a sentiment based on the injunction of the apostle Paul against taking fellow Christians to court (1 Cor. 6:1–2). This is arguably a misapplication of the text because a Christian agency is not only a charity; it is also an employer which is legally bound by employment law to observe the statutory rights of its employees. An employment tribunal might help a Christian organization to be more 'Christian'.

How Much Progress Are We Making?

That said, it is not all doom and gloom. For instance, in June 2020 a survey by Ipsos Mori, conducted after the Black Lives Matter protests, showed that two thirds of those polled supported the need for social justice and were optimistic that the UK would become a more tolerant and diverse society within a decade. When asked if someone must be white to be British, 84% said a firm 'no' – an increase from 55% in 2009.[39] The well-known 'Rivers of Blood' speech in 1968 was given by Conservative MP Enoch Powell, who was originally part of the open invitation for migrants to come to Britain for work. He later changed his mind and prophesied that mass migration would be catastrophic.[40] While the prediction held elements of truth, such as was seen in the 1981 riots in Brixton and elsewhere, these were not cases of white-on-black violence and they were less about race and more about social deprivation. In spite of this 'prophecy', there are some green shoots of change. For instance, Enoch Powell's former constituency office (Wolverhampton South) has become a multicultural community centre and, at the time of writing, the incumbent MP is a female of Caribbean descent. Also, laws now exist which ban 'incitement to racial hatred'.

However, despite improvements, racist incidents, both verbal and physical, have continued in sport,[41] among children[42] and in public places.[43] A high-profile example is the black Labour MP Diane Abbott, who reported in 2017 that over the previous few years (largely since the Brexit Referendum in 2016), she and her office staff had been receiving obscene racist abuse and death threats, on the basis that 'black people don't belong in politics'.[44]

It seems the spirit of the age says: 'Why should *they* matter to me when I don't matter to *them*?' The way of Jesus would respond: 'They *should* matter to you because they matter to God', which is the punchline to the parable of the Good Samaritan, an iconic symbol of the Christly response to people who are different, including those of a Muslim family heritage. So before we jump to any activism, we need to scrutinize our heart and repent of any unconscious racism.

In a climate of 'cancelling' negative symbols of the past, such as slavery, it seems valid to ask whether anti-racist protesters would also like to remove the statue of John Newton, who was a well-known slave trader. He converted to Christ, became a Christian minister, and joined the Christian campaigner William Wilberforce in his successful efforts to abolish slavery. Newton's legacy includes the hymn 'Amazing Grace', which made him the patron saint of people who discover they are 'a wretch', in need of redemption. Reverend Giles Fraser spots this irony and describes the current climate as one of 'furious moral vigilantism'. The politically correct zealots 'trawl through . . . public utterances' to condemn, shame and destroy anyone who is perceived to be an opponent in 'the high court of Twitter'.[45] Fraser concludes:

> Morality without forgiveness or redemption is a frightening, persecutory business. Part of the problem with the cancel culture of modern identity politics is that it makes the confession of sins so much more difficult to achieve . . . how can we all confront the various forms of racism, sexism, homophobia and so on that we harbour within, when the consequences of any form of public admission are devastating and toxic? . . . Cancel culture makes us . . . publicly pretend we are better than we are. It turns us all into liars . . . [who] point the finger at others in the hope of misdirecting the anger of the crowd.[46]

We now move on to follow this issue into the next chapter where we will analyse the current atmosphere of abuse that has developed, due to factors such as the pressure to repress individual views. This repression has acted like the weights on a pressure cooker preventing the normal escape of steam. This is a product of political correctness, which is a minefield to be navigated carefully; this is where we go next.

6

Mount Correct

Impacts of weaponized political correctness on society, church, and other faith groups

Don't curse the darkness. Light a candle.
Attributed to Confucius

In this chapter we define and describe 'political correctness' (PC), outlining how it came about, its positive upside and its pernicious downside. We analyse the effect on various sectors of society when its zealots use coercion to shut down discussion and resist critical thinking. We analyse how PC can hinder social cohesion by blocking healthy public interaction, and suggest ways to navigate our way in a climate of PC etiquette.

Mount Correct is the blockage posed by 'political correctness' (PC). It is easy to miss the influence of PC on the interaction between non-Muslims and Muslims. Although not immediately obvious, there are some crucial implications, which can be positive when helping us to be more courteous, but it can be negative when weaponized to achieve an agenda. If we fail to navigate this, interaction becomes strained and complicated. Allow me to explain.

What Is PC?

The PC influence has swept the western world relatively quickly, but its social impact seems to be on a par with major paradigm shifts, such as the creation of the internet by Vinton Cerf and Bob Kahn. Like the internet, PC has an 'upside' and a 'downside', depending on how it is used. The positive side of PC is that it has given us a standard of social etiquette to protect the rights and well-being of minority groups who may otherwise be marginalized, disadvantaged or discriminated against.[1] One positive outcome is gender-inclusive language and equality laws.

The core concept of PC is a western equivalent of the 'social contract' (written or unwritten) which is used in all societies to regulate communal behaviour and create a balance between 'rights' and 'responsibilities' for the common good, rather like a social highway code. This was enshrined in the Judeo-Christian heritage from Old Testament times, where social justice was protected so individuals had civil 'rights' that were balanced by civic 'responsibilities'. These two were held in tension by the community to ensure the well-being of *all* its members, including immigrants and the socially vulnerable: 'He defends the cause of the fatherless and the widow, and loves the foreigner residing among you, giving them food and clothing' (Deut. 10:18). It is possible that this is where Karl Marx (who was Jewish) derived his 'socialist' vision.

In the New Testament, Jesus Christ and his apostles focus on the same principles, which were to be modelled for wider society by the Christian community: 'Religion that God our Father accepts as pure and faultless is this: to look after orphans and widows in their distress' (Jas 1:27) and 'Be wise in the way you act towards outsiders; make the most of every opportunity. Let your conversation be always full of grace, seasoned with salt, so that you may know how to answer everyone' (Col. 4:5–6). This is how Christians are to serve society as moral 'salt' and spiritual 'light' (Matt. 5:13–16), and as 'yeast' which affects 'the whole batch of dough' (Gal. 5:9). It is a lifestyle of *grace*-speech as opposed to *hate*-speech. In this way, the early followers of Christ were PC before it was fashionable.

The Dark Side of PC

However, the negative outcome of PC is its flawed underbelly, which was developed by secularists who took the original concept and decoupled it from its ethical roots in the Judeo-Christian tradition. If the core concept of PC is not new, it must be argued that the current iteration of it is. I will call the negative use of PC 'PC *rules*', rather than PC etiquette. PC rules are an aspect of a broader philosophy, now called 'identity politics', which emerged during the 1960s and 1970s among existentialist philosophers such as Michel Foucault.[2] I find it ironic that, although Foucault was a secularist European, his thinking appears to have been shaped (at least in part) by the Judeo-Christian heritage he grew up with but came to reject. He claimed that *all* human belief systems are shaped by the prevailing power-structures more than by 'truth'. What he seemed to be saying was that this is the case for everyone except himself and that his thinking is uniquely free of the subjective influence of the Christendom he grew up with. This is another example of the proverbial goldfish unaware it is swimming in the element of water because it has never known anything else.

Foucault's conclusions were a form of intellectual anarchy because he was advocating the deconstruction of all 'false' distinctions in order to 'liberate' people from traditional patterns of thinking. He even saw the notion of maleness and femaleness as a social construct which should be dismantled. This is at the root of the 'transgender' movement.

People analyse PC differently; for some it is the 'coming of age' of western civilization, while for others it is evidence of a creaking civilization that must be fixed before it is too late. Many Bible-believing Christians see the dark side of PC as a sign that society is in the 'last days' before the return of Jesus Christ, and that we are in an era when 'some will abandon the faith and follow deceiving spirits and things taught by demons' (1 Tim. 4:1–3). While I have sympathy with that view, it should not detract from the fact that our task is to counter such thinking. It may be a 'sign of the times' but we are also called to address the 'need of the hour'.

Why and How Did PC Spread So Fast?

The speed at which PC has spread can be attributed to the fact that it resonates best with nations that have the Judeo-Christian heritage in their psyche and which in the post-Christendom era were looking for secular expressions of familiar values. This made PC more acceptable to academia, the media, and government departments. Hence the swift legislation of aspects of PC etiquette. When we take a step back, we can trace the spread of PC along the following lines.

1. The raw ingredients of the Foucault philosophy were consolidated by ideologically driven academics and university lecturers in disciplines such as education, the humanities and the social sciences. These champions often had a conflict of interest in their research because they themselves were products of the very social issues in question, including divorce, single-parent families and alternative lifestyles, and were even victims of abuse.

2. From there, PC gathered momentum to the point where it became effectively a form of 'social contagion', which I am defining as an 'infectious' influence which convinces people to believe and behave in illogical ways, even when it bypasses the traditional fact-based *evidence*. The latter is replaced with a feelings-based *ideology*, which is an ideal that rejects inconvenient facts and reacts to being challenged. This has contributed to a 'snowflake' culture where people are fragile and must not be upset. Analysts suggest this has caused the crisis we face in the teaching of critical thinking to students.

3. At this point it became clear that maverick PC 'zealots' were emerging, with an agenda that was atheist and even fascist. When they show themselves in public, such zealots are often strident, opinionated and bullying, with little tolerance of dissenting voices. In this way, they have been prolific in weaponizing PC rules as a means of gaining social control.

4. The public use of social media has become an all-pervasive vehicle for the spreading and monitoring of PC. It is used to encourage tribalism, a herd instinct, online abuse, bullying, 'wokeness',

'cancel culture' and 'trolling'. All this has helped to create a culture of 'groupthink'.

5. PC rules have been taken up by media executives, who have championed them and required them to be followed by news anchors, journalists, interviewers, politicians and celebrities; in fact, anyone in public life can get their knuckles wrapped or be formally disciplined or even sacked by line management for a breach of PC rules.

The Strident Use of PC

Strident PC is an iron fist (rules) in a velvet glove (etiquette) – or in biblical language a 'wolf in sheep's clothing'. This subtle switch often confuses people who talk about PC, because they are not specific about which expression of it they mean: the benign and reasonable aspect which builds on the Judeo-Christian heritage for the common good, or the strident aspect which seeks to control and damage others to create a society in its own image.

Growing up in the 1970s as a person of colour, I was acutely aware of the more absurd PC rules. Take, for instance, my schooldays when the word 'blackboard' was banned as racist and replaced by 'chalkboard', without asking for the opinion of black people. When I was a student in teacher training, I noticed that the word 'whiteboard' was *not* seen as racist (I assumed that white people too had not been canvassed for their opinion on that either). Looking back, it seems everyone (including education authorities) was feeling their way; whoever spoke loudest and sounded confident was assumed to be authoritative, but they were just guessing. I have never met a black person yet who was offended by referring to a blackboard by its true colour. It seemed race was the elephant in the room and people were required to tiptoe around it in clumsy ways, such as describing black people as 'coloured' – which, by the way, *is* offensive to black people, because it has a direct link to the former apartheid terminology of South Africa.

My formative years felt a bit like that well-known episode of the TV comedy *Fawlty Towers* where hotel owner Basil Fawlty kept insisting

'Don't mention the war' due to the presence of German guests. One black woman told me: 'The word "coloured" comes across as a clumsy attempt to be polite; it's as if I, as a black person, do not know I am black, and I may be offended if someone tells me I am.'

The academic and social commentator Jordan Peterson described this sort of PC as the 'lovechild of two ideologies, "postmodernism" and "Marxism"' (i.e. the velvet glove and the iron fist).[3] For Peterson, all ideologies see society as operating in one of two ways, 'tribal' (i.e. corporate) or 'individual' (i.e. individualistic). The individualistic view takes the individual (*not* the group) as the basic unit of society. This reflects the postmodern world view, which is more self-oriented, emphasizing the individual's feelings, whereby it is their *right* to be free to define themselves without being stereotyped or beholden to others or having a *responsibility* to them.

The 'tribal' or corporate view of society is the pattern in many cultures, particularly in the Global South, where primacy is given to the group, clan or tribe, in the cultural sense, to the Ummah (global Muslim community) in the Islamic sense, or to the 'party' in the Communist sense. Peterson uses the work of naturalist Jane Goodall to illustrate a similar group dynamic in chimpanzee societies, where chimps observe group rules and patrol the boundaries of their territory where those rules apply. There is an 'us and them' atmosphere in which they will attack any chimp that violates this space if it is not a member of the group.

It is easy to see the parallel in human cultures where adherents of a belief system want it to be exported to wider society, including fundamentalist Christians or fundamentalist Muslims who may wish to see society become an extension of themselves. This is certainly true of strident PC zealots who mark out their territory and then police it by naming and shaming those who violate the rules.

Strident PC as the Thought Police

It seems to me that most fair-minded people will be able to affirm the positive aspects of PC values when it is for the common good, while challenging the negative aspects, which become socially destructive. The classic profile of a PC zealot is found in the following categories: atheists, secularists, ultra-liberals, politically left-wing groups, anarchic dismantlers of the status quo, and any who see themselves as being en route to a society in their image.

The strident form of PC creates a hierarchy among minority groups, with gender and sexuality ranked higher and faith affiliation ranked lower. This potentially sets one minority at odds with another, which in itself damages our prized 'social cohesion'.

Even high-profile celebrities can be attacked online and in the media; for instance Milo Yiannopoulos, the British-born, US-based, right-wing political writer and commentator. He is the strident PC warriors' worst nightmare because they do not know where to place him nor how to respond to his anti-PC views. They choose instead to attack him personally for being un-PC, even though he ticks more of their PC boxes than they do. By this I am referring to the fact that he has Greek/Jewish dual ethnicity, he is a practising Catholic, *and* he is gay and married to a black American man.

Transgenderism

As a gay man, Yiannopoulos challenges some of the transgender assumptions and has experienced vitriolic attack for doing so. Prominent women (gay and 'straight') are also attacked for holding similar views, including Germaine Greer (feminist and women's rights campaigner), Jenny Murray (veteran BBC presenter), J.K. Rowling (the Harry Potter author) – who was publicly disowned by the young actors who were helped to stardom and wealth by the film franchise of her work[4] – and Abigail Shrier (*Wall Street Journal* columnist and author of the book *Irreversible Damage: The Transgender Craze Seducing Our Daughters* [2020]).[5] These women have been branded as 'TERFs' (Trans-Exclusionary Radical Feminists) and even threatened with physical violence.

According to the Christian Institute,[6] over the past decade, the wing of the National Health Service (NHS) known as the Gender

Identity Development Service has seen a 3,000% increase in referrals from children who claim to have gender dysphoria, and a school in Brighton reports forty cases and pupils grooming other pupils to follow their lead. While some argue this is happening due to easier access to help and a sympathetic social climate, experts are now identifying what is being called a 'social contagion' (i.e. a craze) among young people, due to factors such as difficulty adjusting to puberty, peer pressure from friends who have identified as transgender, increased online activity beforehand, being mentored by friends about what to say to a doctor or therapist (and that it's OK to lie), as well as how to use a 'suicide narrative' to convince parents.

The black lesbian rapper Dotty Charles hosts the Radio 1Xtra *Breakfast Show* and has challenged strident forms of PC in her book *Outraged* in which she calls out those who are weaponizing social media by what she terms 'clicktivism' or 'hashtag activism'. She denounces the mantra 'I am offended', saying it is a poor shorthand for 'I have principles'. This is known as 'virtue signalling', where an assailant claims the moral high ground – a behaviour Dotty Charles sees as 'shallow self-righteousness'. She accuses strident PC zealots of settling for a 'half-hearted and lazy substitute for the sort of action that changes things', saying that it is all too easy to 'stand with the mob without actually contributing to the cause in question'.[7]

PC Impact on Comedy

The American talk show host Bill Maher defined strident PC attitudes as a 'cult of offence'. By this he means the 'moral posturing which elevates *sensitivity* over the pursuit of truth'.[8] To be offended seems to automatically confer moral superiority on the one who is offended (i.e. the 'offendee'). It can never be their fault, so their discomfort must be the fault of the one who offended them (i.e. the 'offender'), who is pressured to apologize and to admit that it is they who need help to cure their 'phobia'. This process has introduced a licence for social bullying, social control, and nastiness in public discourse.

Take, for instance, the British actor Laurence Fox, who appeared on the BBC 1 TV panel show *Question Time* and argued for the rights of white males to be allowed to have a view on an issue without being unfairly caricatured and labelled by strident PC zealots as 'racist' or 'sexist', or as suffering from so-called 'white privilege'.[9] Others in the entertainment industry also challenge the 'tribal' view of society as espoused by strident PC rules, such as several comedians who see themselves as being among the last ones to hold out against the pressure to conform. They describe PC rules as 'the preoccupation of guilty white liberals' and 'intolerance, masquerading as the epitome of tolerance and fairness'.[10] One of them, the actor and writer Stephen Fry, said: 'We all want the "golden rule" [see Matt. 7:12] and the abolition of bigotry . . . but my ultimate objection to PC is not that it is preachy, self-righteous, shaming, and an assertion without evidence – it just does not work. It prefers to be "right" more than to be effective.'[11]

PC Impact on Muslims

The same Muslim leader who alerted me to the existence of the word 'hegemony' (see chapter 4) also complained to me about the use of PC in ways that are unhelpful to Muslims because it makes it look like Muslims are demanding things while it can be the PC zealots who are deciding how Muslims *should* be asking to be treated. Putting words into the mouth of the Muslim communities can create ill-feeling among the wider public. Here are some incidents which illustrate this happening:

• PC rules require the public to be 'tolerant' towards Muslims, which sounds helpful, until we realize that the dictionary definition of the word 'tolerate' is to 'endure' or to 'put up with' something. This is not the stuff of genuine social cohesion. The situation has worsened because the popular phraseology has changed again from 'tolerate' to 'approve' (or even 'endorse'). This is worrying because the rule becomes a requirement to comply with something, whether we agree with it or not, which brings us back to the 'thou shalt' draconian nature of strident PC rules.[12]

- We went through a phase where some primary schools stopped holding Nativity plays in case it offended Muslims. Although for some this appears to be a ruse to obliterate Christian markers from national life, let us take it at face value and assume it was well-meant. The idea of banning Nativity plays baffles mainstream Muslims because the virgin birth of Christ is a tenet of the Islamic religion (Qur'an 19:121; 66:12).[13] One Muslim leader in the north of England made this point to me, then added with a wry smile: 'We believe in the virgin birth of Christ, which is more than some bishops believe.' Ouch! When such strident forms of PC rules are taken to their logical conclusion, they become absurd.

- In England in 2020, Ramadan, Passover and Easter fell during the Covid lockdown and all faith groups had to forgo any religious celebrations. For instance, the Jewish community could not mark Passover and the Seder meal, while Christians could not observe their Easter vigil. That said, there were some successful requests made to local authorities, which granted special permission to broadcast the Muslim call to prayer (*azaan*) outside the mosques on each Friday in Ramadan and at the start of Eid (*eid-ul-fitr*), which marks the end of the fast.[14] These well-meaning local authorities were apparently unaware that Muslims already have apps which do the job of linking them to the wider community at their times of prayer. Such preferential treatment by city councillors is what provokes concern and even ill-feeling against the Muslim community, rather than the astute and opportunistic few who know how to play the PC 'victim card' to press for special privileges on behalf of the entire Muslim community. This too hinders social cohesion.

- Strident PC rules are even coming across to Muslims as patronizing. The *New Statesman* reported that, in recent years, there have been attempts by 'politically correct' local authorities to downplay or even suppress Christmas. For example, Birmingham City

Council tried to create a new seasonal celebration called 'Winterval', while Luton opted for a Harry Potter-themed festival of lights. Such decisions appear to be motivated by a fear that overt displays of Christian faith might offend British Muslims. Either way, it is a symbol of 'religious illiteracy' because the virgin birth of Jesus Christ is a tenet of Islamic belief. The fear is therefore misplaced. The notable Muslim cleric Sheikh Ibrahim Mogra has led the Muslim Council of Britain's interfaith relations committee and concurs. He said that the suggestion to change the name of Christmas was 'ridiculous' and that Britain is great at celebrating the diverse religious festivals of its various faith communities. He went on to say that the festivals' names should not be changed, and they should all be celebrated. Mogra urged Muslims to engage in an outward and public celebration of Jesus, in particular his birth, to reflect the private reverence that Muslims have for him.[15]

It seems unfair when clumsy media coverage gives the public the impression that *all* Muslims are intolerant and are always asking for special treatment, while behind the scenes it is the PC zealots who are responsible.

PC Impact on Society

The unthinking application of PC does damage to social cohesion, as Nazir Afzal points out. He is a barrister and a former Chief Crown Prosecutor for the North West of England, and he has a Pakistani Muslim family background. Afzal reflects on the damage done in his region by muddled thinking about PC requirements. The problem started when a network of Pakistani taxi drivers formed a grooming gang to pimp and sexually abuse underage and socially vulnerable white girls. The gang members were emboldened to continue operating unchallenged for several years, because the police, the media and the local authorities were all reluctant to act for *fear* of being branded 'racist' and 'Islamophobic'. The abuse was ultimately challenged by a whistle-blower who came forward to expose the crimes.[16] The paralysis in this case was experienced by people who felt out of their depth and so were intimidated by the thought of being targeted for PC reprisals, which could have entailed losing their job.

Another example cited by Afzal is the unusual 'spike' in Covid-19 virus infections in the north-west of England among South Asian communities. Afzal comments on a PC skirmish in the press involving the white local Conservative MP, Craig Whittaker, who said publicly that the majority of the people breaking social-distancing rules were black and South Asian. The PC reaction was instant and vitriolic; for example the black MP and Labour Party equalities spokesperson Marsha de Cordova said that the statement was 'disgraceful' and that it was an act of 'overt racism' for which the prime minister should discipline Whittaker.[17]

As a barrister, Afzal assessed the facts and confirmed that Whittaker's claim was correct, but then went on to explain that the reason for the spike in black and South Asian deaths was due to these ethnicities being genetically and/or physiologically more susceptible to the effects of the virus. In Afzal's opinion this cannot be helped, but it can and must be *managed* to mitigate the real challenges, which are cultural, sociological and economic as follows:

1. These ethnicities tend to have a lower socio-economic status than other communities (i.e. they tend to live, shop and work more cheek-by-jowl), which may be an underlying social justice issue.
2. They have different cultural patterns (e.g. multigenerational-occupancy housing, which helps take pressure off local authorities for care of the elderly), and extended family members may live close by in multiple 'bubbles' which blur the line drawn to prevent household mixing. This can only be managed from *within* the community, but government had failed to collaborate with Asian volunteers who were working hard to interpret some confusing official guidelines, both linguistically and culturally. A source on the

ground told me they had asked for collaboration but felt sidelined by government.

3. Many indigenous white Britons were confused by government messaging about Covid-19 transmission, so it was inevitable that some South Asians would struggle to understand it when English is their second or even third language.

In my view, Afzal's explanation was true to PC etiquette, and the vitriolic overreactions were examples of the negative application of PC rules in a social climate where those who shout loudest are assumed to be in the right, sometimes to the detriment of the common good.

If South Asian Muslims can be overlooked, what about black Muslims – who are sometimes referred to as the 'twice black'?

PC Impact on Black People

After the killing of George Floyd in the USA, strident PC zealots in the Black Lives Matter organization assumed the moral high ground, which they believed gave them the right to destroy anything that depicted past racial oppression. They toppled statues of famous white people and forced the deletion of previous episodes of certain TV programmes. They banned films, such as *Gone with the Wind*, and tried to ban popular songs such as the rugby anthem 'Swing Low, Sweet Chariot', because it emerged in the slave era. The Caribbean observer Trevor Phillips, himself a tsar of positive PC values, warned that, however well-intentioned, this was a step too far because in the process it could obliterate black history itself. If we must never forget the Holocaust lest it ever happen again, why are we determined to forget the black struggle? This, says Phillips, is to miss the point and it will ultimately be counterproductive. We may not agree with everything Phillips says, but he seemed to champion the best of PC values when he tweeted to the effect that things go too far when even the song 'Swing Low, Sweet Chariot' is called into question and attempts are made to 'cancel' it as a celebration in the sport of rugby. The song was written after the American Civil War by a freed slave who was referring to the 'underground slave railway' that took enslaved people to freedom. Apparently the song was popularized by the black American Fisk Jubilee Singers, has been sung at black funerals as well as civil rights demonstrations, and was honoured by Congress. It was also a favourite of Paul Robeson, Louis Armstrong and Martin Luther King Jr. The song was last banned in Germany in 1939 and now 'woke' culture is seeking to ban it. Phillip's point here is that black people's own culture is being 'cancelled'. He asks us all to take a deep breath before eliminating black lives from history.

PC Impact on Christians

Strident forms of PC can be intimidating for active Christians, who may start to doubt their voice in public discourse for fear of being targeted as bigots. For example, I was personally set up and ambushed in an interview I gave for a Channel 4 TV documentary, which subtly twisted both ends of the spectrum of Christian interaction with Muslims, the 'conciliatory' and the 'confrontational' (see chapter 9).

In the documentary, the combative Christian debaters at Speakers' Corner in Hyde Park, London, were portrayed as bombastic bullies, and those involved in social engagement were portrayed as having a hidden agenda to proselytize Muslims. Both caricatures were an intentionally skewed snapshot that was taken through a strident PC lens. The film makers ignored the views of Muslims, and one observer described the programme's take on social engagement as an attempt to cynically rubbish the concept of the Good Samaritan.

The programme caused many Christians to move away from media exposure altogether, which is part of the corrosive effect of strident PC on Christian confidence in themselves and what they stand for. This has come out on occasions during cross-cultural awareness seminars I conduct for churches. Some evangelicals have even asked: 'What right do we have to engage in gospel conversations with a Muslim when they have a faith of their own?' If this is the case for everyday Christians, what about church leaders?

PC Impact on Church Leaders

Church leaders, even denominational heads, have said to me: 'Interaction with people of other faiths is a *specialist* issue, so we leave it to the "professionals" who know what they're doing.' A leader of a globally known Australian megachurch told me: 'We prefer to do nothing, rather than make mistakes and offend people.' A British church leader confided: 'If it went wrong, our church would be in the news for all the wrong reasons.' I take such comments as evidence of the subtle erosion of Christian confidence due to the joint influence of postmodern relativism and the policing of strident PC rules.

Christianity in Public Space

That said, I am not suggesting that Christians should communicate in the public sphere without adequate preparation. For example, in 2019 (before the Covid-19 virus), a media storm hit both sides of the Atlantic about statements made in public space by Franklin Graham, son of the late great evangelist Billy Graham. Assertions were made on social media, including 'AIDS is a divine judgement', 'Islam is evil' and 'same-sex marriage is orchestrated by Satan'.[18] My point in raising this is not to debate whether such statements are true or untrue, nor whether we agree with them or are horrified by them; I am merely highlighting what the strident PC zealots did with these comments, which did not help Franklin Graham or the Christian cause.

The fallout from the statements came later when Graham was planning his 2020 British preaching tour of seven cities: the events were forced to be cancelled because the proprietors of each of the intended public venues refused to honour the bookings. There is a maxim that it is possible to say the *wrong* thing in the right way and retain the hearer, and it is possible to say the *right* thing in the wrong way and lose the hearer. Whatever Christians say, they must learn to be as 'wise as serpents' and 'harmless as doves', as those who live 'as sheep in the midst of wolves' (Matt. 10:16 NKJV); this means becoming communication-savvy in the current climate.

Christians on Social Media Platforms

This is the learning curve that Christians face in the post-Covid era where live streaming online is set to mushroom in a 'church without walls'. As Christian activity increases online and on social platforms, what is said can be picked up by *anyone*, anywhere in the world. I personally see this as good discipline for Christian communicators who are now able to serve the current context, rather than just speaking among themselves.

I say all this because I know Christian pioneers on Facebook and YouTube who have found themselves subjected to the scrutiny of strident PC rules. Some have fallen foul of this and been taken down for 'unacceptable' content, that is, unacceptable to the media giants, rather than to most fair-minded people. For example, Jay Smith, an American who has brought a combative style to public engagement online with radical Muslims, reports that he is regularly blocked by YouTube, which claims he is in breach of their 'contents policy'. Smith reports on this in a newsletter (cited here with permission):

Most of my videos uploaded this year have been . . . deemed as 'inappropriate' by YouTube.

It is becoming increasingly difficult to say anything critical of Islam in the West, due to political correctness or retaliation by Muslims [who] deem [it] is injurious to their faith. It is only a matter of time before all channels which critique Islam are shut down and the only criticism permitted will be Islamic channels, which engage in personal diatribes and vitriol against Christianity [and] personal insults against those who defend it publicly. This double standard is echoed across social media platform[s], suggesting those in authority over Western media are either ignorant of the double-standard or are fearful of Muslim retaliation. You-Tube must not succumb to 'political correctness' and permit freedom of speech [to defend] Christianity publicly [and] hold Islam accountable.[19]

Another online debater with radical Muslims is David Brown, who experiences similar censorship for raising the issue of the persecution of Christian minorities in Muslim lands.[20] Brown is compelling but can be provocative. He might be helped by the admonition of the apostle Peter who says: 'if you should suffer for what is right, you are blessed . . . [Keep] a clear conscience . . . for it is better, if it is God's will, to suffer for doing good than for doing evil' (1 Pet. 3:14–17). To achieve this, the constraints might include the following:

- Make sure we do not do something to deserve the opposition we may get.
- Model the best of PC etiquette.
- 'Fish for people' (Matt. 4:19) by knowing the PC habitat they live in to avoid driving the fish away.
- Be aware of the five legal equalities: 'age', 'race', 'gender', 'religion' and 'sexual orientation'.
- Bear in mind that anything we say online may set off unnecessary reactions at home and abroad; for example, after a Danish cartoonist produced a series of illustrations of Muhammad in September 2005, 250 people were killed in protests in Pakistan.
- Be 'as shrewd as snakes and as innocent as doves' (Matt. 10:16) and use words that are 'gracious, seasoned with salt' (Col. 4:6 ESV).

PC and Christian Theology

An impact of the PC climate is that Christians have been presented with the opportunity to focus less on internal debates and more on playing catch-up with the pressing theological issues of our day, some of which come to us courtesy of PC sentiments. Whatever our personal view on the ethical issues of our time, it has become a fact of life that we live in a more attitudinally *open* society, which periodically poses meaty theological issues to 'the church', who are expected to speak into national discourse, but do not. The issues have included divorce, female ordination, and same-sex attraction (both in marriage and in 'ministry'). Sexual ethics is likely to remain on the national agenda for the next decade or so, as the pastoral issues come to the fore among committed Christians who are same-sex attracted (SSA), including some clergy and high-profile worship leaders. This has been unsettling, but it might help to know that such theological work has been happening periodically throughout church history.

So far, there are two main positions in the sexuality debate. First, that SSA individuals should 'come out' and remain celibate; a position held by evangelical Christians such as those in the Living Out network.[21] The second view is held by evangelical Christians who include SSA Christians (and couples) in their fellowships and hold them to the *same* biblical standards expected of heterosexual couples, including courtship and monogamous marriage – a position held by evangelical Christians such as those linked with the Reformation Project.[22]

With regard to the 'transgender' issue, the pastoral implications are clearly huge, and people may well turn to churches for help. The additional complexities are likely to prompt collaboration with psychologists and ethicists because this issue defies categorization within the Abrahamic faiths (i.e. the Judeo-Christian tradition and Islam) where there is little to no relevant scriptural material to grapple with. We know that there are already profound misgivings in this area among medical clinicians and psychologists, some of whom are challenging the fast-tracking of young people for transgender surgery, because they fear the process is being driven more by ideology than science. The UK government recently declined to respond to the pressure of the PC zealots when it announced in September 2020 that professional checks and balances were to be introduced before a diagnosis of gender dysphoria is accepted.

PC and Christian Mission Organizations

In Covid-19 language, Christian mission organizations have some 'underlying health conditions' which make them vulnerable to negative PC scrutiny because they are preoccupied with *viability* rather than *relevance* and are in denial of that fact. The following points show where the blind spot seems to have set in:

- The role of Mount Imperial (upon which the older mission organizations were predicated) was dismantled from the 1960s onwards and churches in the former colonies (known as the 'mission field') became autonomous, prompting mission agencies to have to discover what they are now for.
- Access to many countries has diminished greatly or closed, so what the mission groups used to be for has been made more difficult to maintain.
- The day of the *career* mission worker is over and the generation that supported them is passing away; a new funding model is therefore required, but this is impossible within their current 'wineskin'.
- Western 'sending nations' are now sites of *cross-cultural* witness as local churches find themselves on a new cross-cultural frontline.
- A misunderstanding exists between the mission agency, which looks to the local church for funding to send people 'over there', and the local church, which looks for partnership to engage with the same ethnic peoples who are now living 'over here'.
- Mission agencies restrict their focus and theological reflection to issues traditionally within their frame of reference, rather than dealing with the trending theological issues of the day, which will have a 'make-or-break' impact on what they do.

The full scope of the Great Commission of Christ will always remain *global* (geographically) and *pan-cultural* (racially) – focusing on 'all nations' (Matt. 28:19). However, the question of who tackles what, and where, depends on the needs at any time. We now live in a post-colonial era where Christian mission is no longer 'from the West to the rest' as it was in the colonial era, but now operates from everywhere to everywhere, because the 'ends of the earth' have come to live in every 'Jerusalem' (Acts 1:8).

Another 'underlying health condition' that compromises western mission agencies is their vulnerability to attack from aggressive PC zealots who have a 'bone to pick' with colonialism and religion, seeing such agencies as anachronistic remnants of a bygone era. They are seen by some, as behaving like global commercial companies in a new form of colonialism (i.e. *neo*-colonialism), as well as espousing the morals of a past age. Such agencies are operating in a climate where the UK government's Office for National Statistics (ONS) indicated, in 2018, that 7.9% of Britons identified as 'same-sex attracted' (SSA).[23] The number of SSA Christian workers currently working with an agency will probably reflect this average but they remain 'closeted'. As time goes on those applying to join an agency do so under revised UK employment laws which forbid discrimination based on sexual orientation. There is an opt-out clause for churches and 'faith-based charities'; however, this point of law has not yet been tested by assertive applicants who may not wish to hide their sexuality.

Another angle on PC pressure is that all charities could be required by some trust funds to tick certain PC boxes to demonstrate what is considered 'good practice'. For example, they may now need to show in their 'annual return' *how* their work is contributing to 'the public good'. The choice of trusts to approach may become limited unless they can produce a position statement on 'proselytization', or 'inducement' to convert, or 'sexuality'. This adds to the subtle pressure to de-emphasize *spiritual* work in favour of *humanitarian* work which is more acceptable (and legally compliant).[24]

Mission agencies face the 'perfect storm' as PC rules and Covid restrictions swirl around them. As a result, Christian charities are left brokering a tension that is not entirely of their own making. The default position can be to become more *managerial* about the mission enterprise, which looks set to default towards relief and development as mission agencies are pressured to portray themselves to Christians as 'conversionist' (to elicit prayer and financial support from donors who perceive the agency to be what it was in bygone years), while portraying themselves to the government and granting trusts as essentially 'humanitarian' agencies with a Christian ethos. In this scenario the injunction to be 'as wise as serpents' collides with 'All you need to say is a simple "Yes" or "No". Otherwise you will be condemned' (Jas 5:12).

PC and the Herd Instinct

Strident PC has become associated with 'groupthink', which thrives on fake news and alternative facts, which distort people's grasp of reality and inspire loyalty to causes they know little about. This was apparent when the reporter Avi Yemini (himself of Jewish heritage) interviewed people with a range of ethnicities who marched in Melbourne, Australia, in breach of the Covid lockdown, to support Black Lives Matter and to protest the killing of George Floyd in the USA.[25] Yemini asked protesters why they knew about George Floyd and were angry enough to protest about a black man being killed in America by a white policeman, yet they had never heard of Justine Damond, a white *Australian* woman, killed in America by a black policeman, while she was standing on her own doorstep, wearing pyjamas.

The answers Yemini got showed the protesters' mindset: they insisted that it was 'because George Floyd was black' and that Justine Damond's killing 'was not as bad'. This seems to be 'groupthink' at its worst. The phenomenon of 'fake news' is now being challenged by a breed of specialists called 'super fact-checkers', part of a service that is springing up to inform the public, governments and business. It includes organizations such as Logically, founded by Lyric Jain; Full Fact, founded by Will Moy; and the non-profit website FactCheck (www.factcheck.org).

Navigating PC Etiquette

I hope we have established that an analysis of PC cannot be binary; to try to make it so would be to create more fake news. PC is neither *all* good nor *all* bad. We do well to take the advice of the apostle Paul, who urges us to be discerning about what is 'true', 'noble', 'right', 'pure', 'lovely', 'excellent' or 'praiseworthy' (Phil. 4:8). We must reserve the right to affirm or reject aspects of PC and, to do that, it can help to ask questions, such as: 'Is this really the sort of society we want?'

This was done by the historian, broadcaster and social commentator David Starkey, who describes himself as an 'atheist' and 'gay'. Speaking on BBC 1's *Question Time*, he referred to PC rules as an 'oppressive liberal morality'. Starkey went on to support the PC rights of a Christian hotelier who had been prosecuted for refusing to assign a double room to a same-sex couple. Starkey said the hotelier should simply have been required by law to put up a sign outside his B&B and online, saying that on faith grounds he and his wife decline the business of gay customers. Starkey concluded to a hushed TV audience: 'We are producing a new tyranny.'[26] You could have heard a pin drop.

When we balance our view of PC etiquette, we leave room for appreciating the positive aspects, as well as recognizing where the strident zealots bury their social landmines. Those Christians who are brave enough to engage in public discourse can learn to navigate the minefield and counteract the nonsense by pointing to a better way, which, when described in a compelling manner, makes sense and is accessible to those who do not share their world view. Jesus showed the way because he knew how far to go when he was breaking social etiquette. For example, when he approached a Samaritan woman at a well in Sychar (John 4), he did so in a calculated way, knowing it was disgraceful for him to interact with a non-Jewish female in an isolated public place. We too can learn to avoid (or at least limit) potential social explosions. I would go further to suggest that Jesus modelled PC etiquette, by balancing 'grace' in his attitude with 'truth' in his actions; that is, 'grace' is both the *message* and the *method* of conveying it.

The technical term for this is *kerygma*, which has been the historic pattern for Christians down the centuries. Martin Accad describes it as a centrist and biblically based approach, which is Christian witness that is Christ-centred rather than Christianity-centred. It is a supra-religious way of interacting that prevents unnecessary friction and helps us avoid interpreting history through the triumphalistic lens of Christendom where the western view is thought to be superior.[27]

Kerygmatic interaction is neither a 'technique' nor a 'strategy', but the balanced *disposition* of 'grace and truth' combined. It also helps keep the door open for ongoing interaction, rather than being only about 'hit-and-run' encounters with people we disagree with. It is about going beyond being mere peace*keepers* (i.e. managing the tensions caused by the mountain blockages) to aspire to become peace-*makers* (i.e. assisting closure to misunderstanding and progress in trusting relationship). This is the sort of society that is in everyone's interest.

We have seen that PC *etiquette* can serve the common good but that strident PC *rules* tend to be driven by our lower human instincts to control others, or to take revenge for something. The opposite side to forced PC is that it provokes, in others, reactions such as aggression, retaliation, territorialism and tribalism. This is coming from a significant section of society because people feel coerced into thinking, acting and saying things they do not want to, even if it is supposed to be for the common good. For these individuals, it feels like being accosted by strangers on the street to give to a charity. Their reaction is that charity is good, but 'I will give to who I want to, so back off!'

In this way, PC (etiquette and rules) have had the unintended consequence of provoking public resentment. This has been festering like a pressure cooker from which steam periodically has to escape, which is precisely what we have been seeing in the form of strident attitudes and verbal invective in the press and online, and even aggression and disorder in the streets.

This is the stuff of the next blockage to healthy social interaction, Mount Strident, which is where we go next.

7

Mount Strident

What sort of society are we becoming?

> You can safely assume that you've created God in your
> own image when it turns out that God hates all the
> same people you do.
>
> Anne Lamott, *Traveling Mercies*[1]

In this chapter we see how public frustration over political correctness has contributed to a popular public revolt for and against issues such as immigration, racism and Islamist violence. We see how this has caused many Muslims to withdraw to avoid abuse – verbal, online and physical. We look at how we can navigate this blockage with a counter-narrative which injects positivity and possibilities for a better future.

Human nature does not take kindly to being told what to do and Mount Strident is a result. It has become a 'social contagion', a counter-reaction to the control of PC 'rules'. It spreads via social media and often relies on 'fake news' to convince people to believe certain things and to behave in illogical ways.

Like a pressure cooker, the pot occasionally reaches boiling point, and strident reactions erupt into the public domain. This is a gift to the tabloid press, which enthusiastically reports abusive behaviour towards minorities, such as Muslims,[2] Jews,[3] black people in sport,[4] MPs (especially female, black or Jewish),[5] the police,[6] and sexual minorities.[7] It could be argued that, since PC rules took hold, the UK has become *more* strident, not less, and that the minority groups which PC was meant to protect have received *worse* treatment, not better. The Brexit debate culminated in the 2019 UK election and became an iconic moment of division which even divided some families, including that of the prime minister Boris Johnson.

What Does 'Strident' Mean?

Words described as 'strident' are loud or harsh, whether spoken or written, whether expressed overtly or covertly (i.e. bluntly or subtly). If we take a step back, we see that any sentiment we express outwardly is first conceived inwardly as a mental storyline of how we believe the world should work. The technical term is a 'narrative', which can be positive, neutral or negative. There seems to be an all-pervasive *negative* narrative about Muslims. An example of it was told to me by a Muslim woman in the form of a joke that does the rounds in Muslim communities:

> An old lady was walking in the local park when a stray dog approached and began to be aggressive to her. A young Muslim man immediately moved in to get between the old lady and the dog. The dog bit the Muslim while he was escorting the old lady to safety. When the story was reported in the local newspaper, the headline was 'Muslim Bites Woman!'

Who Is Most Prone to Be Strident?

A good place to start to answer the above question is with an insight by David Goodhart, who describes two mindsets that shape our attitude. The first is held by people who find their identity somewhere specific (i.e. the 'somewheres'), and the second by those who find their identity anywhere (i.e. the 'anywheres').[8]

On the one hand, the 'somewhere' people are more likely to adopt a strident attitude towards immigrants in general because they have a genuine love of the traditional notion of Britain as predominantly 'white', without going as far as being nationalist or personally racist. They are more likely to still live and work within a short radius of where they were born, and tend to hold traditional family values shaped by Christianity as it was understood in the colonial era. They may have genuine concerns about immigration because it poses a threat to their sense of rootedness. The most strident of the 'somewheres' might be interested in joining a 'far-right' group, which might tend towards actual hostility regarding issues such as immigration.

On the other hand, the 'anywheres' tend to look towards education and achievement, which makes them more geographically mobile. This exposes them to life in urban centres, where they may become even more socially mobile and also find themselves exposed to a more naturally multicultural environment. They tend to be more 'liberal' in outlook, which makes them less concerned by immigration or pluralism, more open to a globalized world view, more accepting of the 'other' and less threatened by diversity. Goodhart reports that in the UK this category has grown from being 6% of the population (fifty years ago) to being around 50% today.

Stridency and Negative Narratives

One of the biggest negative narratives of our time is about Muslims, which is why they are so often unfairly targeted for strident reaction. The Runnymede Trust published a survey in 1999, reporting on 'the common public perception that Muslims are *all* the same, foreign to us, barbaric, violent, oppressing women, and a general threat to a civilized society'. This sat well with the government's earlier tendency to define 'Islamophobia' as 'a type of racism', a definition enshrined in the Equality Act of 2010.[9] This conflates race and religion, which some feel undermines the accepted legal definitions of racism so is thought to add confusion, undermine free speech, and fail to address sectarian hatred.

As a result, Islamophobia was responded to with 'Westophobia' among some Muslims whose *fear* was the perceived decadence, materialism, morality of convenience, and secular godlessness found in western societies. There is no easy solution to this two-way tension, which is why the journey to social cohesion is proving to be such a long and winding road – making books like this one still necessary.

Any negative narrative takes time to dislodge because it appears to be self-evidently true. Such narratives can only be overturned as fresh information comes in. This can be as disturbing for us as it was for Saul of Tarsus on the Damascus Road (Acts 9). His strident attitude was rooted in a *legalistic* religious narrative that was confronted by the alternative narrative of *grace*. The same thing happened to Simon Peter, whose racist narrative was challenged in a dream on a rooftop in Jaffa, where it was replaced by an alternative narrative of God's racial inclusivity (Acts 10).

We need to make sure that our own narrative about Muslims is not infected by the social contagion of fear which often drives strident behaviour. The only way to be certain we are not infected is by ensuring that our narrative is informed by available facts from all angles.

The researcher and journalist Ben White identifies four elements which feed the *negative* narrative about Muslims: concern about 'invasion' (i.e. most Muslims want to swamp us), 'demography' (i.e. most Muslims want to out-birth us); 'treachery' (i.e. most Muslims conspire to turn on us); and 'error' (i.e. most Muslims want to replace Christianity with Islam).[10] If such claims were to be verified it would be a cause for serious concern, not least for many Muslims; so let us pull together some facts about them:

1. *Invasion* (Muslims will swamp us). This asserts that Muslims are 'alien invaders' who will take available jobs, depress the housing market, and swamp public amenities such as schools, the NHS and prisons.[11] The popular perception is that Muslim immigrant families make up around 26% of the population, but the UK Government Cabinet Office says the figure is around 7%. If Muslims were represented in parliament in proportion to their number in the population, there would be around 30 Muslim MPs out of 600 in the House of Commons. In the 2019 general election

the number of Muslim MPs was 18,[12] which seems a fairly static number.

2. *Demography* (most Muslims want to out-birth us). The popular assumption is that Muslims are not only having huge families but doing so as a way of intentionally out-birthing the indigenous Anglo-Saxon population. The facts show that the Muslim birth rate across Europe is in decline. Pakistani and Bangladeshi fertility in the UK dropped from 9.3% in 1971 to 4.9% in 1996. It was less than 3% in 2010.[13] If all immigration to the UK stopped, by 2050 immigrants would be 9.7% of population (i.e. 6.5 million). If medium immigration continues (i.e. at a regular pace rather than involving an influx of further refugees), the number would be 16.7% of population (i.e. 13 million). If a higher rate of immigration continues, according to the Pew Research Center the number would be 17.2% of population (i.e. 13.5 million).[14]

3. *Treachery* (most Muslims will conspire to turn on us). There clearly is an issue with radicals, but British Muslims who support the views of fundamentalists, such as Omar Bakri, Abu Hamza or Anjem Choudary, are about the same number as those white Britons who support ultra-right-wing groups such as the British National Party or the English Defence League. In 2017 the published numbers on the 'jihadi watch list' of the British security services were around 3,500, with up to 25,000 others who were 'of interest'. Such Muslims make up the lunatic fringe of the 3.3 million British Muslims (Office of National Statistics 2018). (More on this in chapter 8.)

We should also remember that during the Covid-19 pandemic, the first ten fatalities among NHS staff were senior consultants (all Muslims) who knowingly risked (and lost) their lives in pursuit of the common good. When Islamists strike in British cities, it is often Muslim physicians who treat the survivors in hospitals.

4. *Error* (most Muslims want to replace Christianity with Islam). Muslim leaders have said to me: 'Our problem is not that Britain is Christian but that it is not Christian enough!' and 'We wish Christians would stand up more for Christianity!' Even when

Muslims make overtures to Christians, they are met with suspicion about their motives; for example, when leading Muslim scholars prepared a document in 2007 called *A Common Word: Love of God and Love of Neighbour* and invited Christians to engage with them on issues of common concern, there was a strong evangelical reaction *against* the process. Senior leaders in the Christian organizations who engaged with this process told me how a significant number of their donors 'punished' them by withdrawing financial support in protest and in a bid to create a sort of doctrinal stance against it.

Perhaps the best response to the above list comes in the words of the prophet Isaiah, who said: 'Do not call everything a conspiracy that other people call a conspiracy [and] do not fear what they fear' (see Isa. 8:12). Let us take this further by going behind the scenes to identify some of the background influences that feed the suspicion.

The Influence of History

Britain's deepest political instincts go back to King Henry VIII when England first stepped away from mainland Europe to develop an identity that has remained 'Protestant' and an 'island nation'. In this way, *religion* and *geography* contributed to the separation from what was then Roman Catholic Europe (see chapter 3). The Reformation created the narrative of an independent and sovereign Britain that has been imbued into the national psyche ever since. The tension came to a head during the Brexit debate, which was about far more than membership of the European Union; namely, it was British *identity* that was at stake in the regaining of borders and sovereignty in its islands and surrounding fishing waters. Immigration (this time, a free flow from Europe) was unnerving the internal narrative of an imperial past (i.e. Mount Imperial) and also assumptions about our nation's status in the world in its own right, and its perceived place in the global pecking order (i.e. Mount Hegemony). Britain's past legacy lives on (partly unconsciously) and causes the national psyche to be conflicted. This is evident when a toxic mix manifests, including grief for former 'glory days', 'post-colonial guilt', and 'hostility' over what the future should look like.

A helpful writer is the American sociologist Philip Jenkins,[15] who pointed out in 2007 that by 2025 the population of continental Europe could (theoretically) include as many as 40 million Muslims out of a total population of 500 million. As part of this trajectory, the people of France, Germany and the Netherlands could be between 20% and 25% of Muslim family stock. For some, this may be a gloomy forecast because, theoretically, Europe could mirror the trend in America, where by 2050 it is expected that white people will have become the 'majority-minority' in the US population; this is due to the projected Hispanic and African American population growth. The USA could end up having no single ethnic group that is larger than 50%.

As a sociologist, Jenkins urges people *not* to panic, pointing instead to the demographic principle we are seeing in the UK. This is that over a handful of generations, immigrant birth rates tend to drop until they approximate that of the indigenous or 'host' population. He points out that birth rates have already shrunk in several Islamic countries and appear to be doing so in Europe. Assuming the security forces keep on top of their vigilance, this also bodes well, because the young Muslims who get radicalized are typically from larger families, which suggests a longer-term possibility (even likelihood) that extremism in European and some Muslim countries could even decline. According to Jenkins, this is just as well because modern European societies do not seem willing to entertain 'institutional' Christianity, and so will certainly *not* tolerate dogmatic or intolerant forms of other faiths.

A positive expectation is that by 2050 several generations of Muslims will have grown up exposed to the secularizing influence of the European social climate and will become increasingly integrated because host societies will have also learned to take better account of the nuances of their citizens with a Muslim heritage. Jenkins sees this sort of government action as a 'courtesy' that should *not* be construed as evidence of the 'Islamization of Europe', as conspiracy theorists would have it.

The Influence of Geography

The colonial era works together with the 'island nation' to make *territory* an issue for Britons. This was a morale booster during the Second World War when Sir Winston Churchill famously said: 'We will fight them on the beaches' (our shores being the last line of defence from invasion). A friend of mine is a volunteer for the Coast Guard on the south coast of England. These days, he is more likely to be asked whether he is watching the horizon for 'foreigners' than for boats in distress. A church leader once said to me in all seriousness: 'God put the English Channel there for a reason.' A similar concern was echoed across mainland Europe when people canvassed by a Chatham House survey said that Europe is 'Christian', and that 'foreigners' should be restricted or kept out altogether.[16]

My own family recognize the island mentality because my father grew up in an island nation of the Caribbean, where questions may be asked such as 'Are we free?' and 'When will we be full?'

The Influence of Identity Politics

We saw in chapter 6 how the relationship between ethnicity, faith affiliation, and identity is a delicate issue that needs nuancing and gets 'lost in translation' whenever official surveys try to analyse it. As human beings, we tend to take our cue from what we see in front of us; so, for instance, East Europeans were among us in the 1990s to the point where, technically speaking, Polish was the second language in Britain. The difference is that, apart from Bosnians, most Muslims are not white and are therefore a more 'visible minority'.

The popular perception is slowly catching up with the fact that, while a white Welsh or Scottish person is not *English* (i.e. not

Anglo-Saxon), they are very much *British* – in the same way that a Muslim is.

When it comes to 'religion', the last national census found that 70% of white Britons identified as 'Christian'. By that they mean *culturally* Christian as opposed to *active* Christian in the biblical sense. In the same way, many identify as 'Muslim', but this tells us little about their actual practice of Islam and a lot about their identity as part of a Muslim community; yet the strident view gives far more political significance to this category. The problem with this tendency is that it suggests that the blanket term 'Muslim' captures the entire Muslim community, assuming that *all* Muslims are one religious and social bloc – they are not. There are almost as many different types of 'Muslim' as there are British Muslims because many are not even religious. Then there is a variety of different expressions of Islam which are informed by the different parts of the world that immigrant families come from.

The respected writer Amir Taheri concurs when he points out the inaccuracy of the western perception that Muslims are the same and that Islam is one amorphous phenomenon. For example, Taheri describes the distinctive expression of Islam among Indian Gujaratis, as distinct from that in Iran, which is as different again in Egypt or Turkey or Somalia. He points out how Islam in different parts of the world tends to take on various hues. For instance, in some it has an Orthodox Christian colouring, and in others an Indian colouring which might even reflect Hindu ideas.[17]

The Influence of Political Agendas

A strident attitude usually reflects a political concern that something needs to be done and no one is doing it. For instance, a Christian leader with a strident attitude told me: 'The government isn't going to do it, so it is our responsibility as Christians to destroy Islam.' This comes across as a politicized form of Christianity and a man-made addendum to the Great Commission of Christ. I find this notion about as far removed from the spirit of the Prince of Peace (Isa. 9:6) as it is possible to get before it stops being Christianity at all. No one ever suggested it was the Church's responsibility to overthrow communism in the twentieth century, so why assume it should be appropriate with Islam in the twenty-first century? The notion echoes imperialism and hegemony.

This attitude also reminds me of Jesus' disciples James and John, whom he called 'sons of thunder' (Mark 3:17) before chiding them with: 'You do not know what manner of spirit you are of' (Luke 9:55 NKJV). They wanted to take matters into their own hands and destroy Samaritan immigrants who had opposed them (Luke 9:51–54). I see this incident as Jesus being *Christly* in the way a good president should be *presidential*. To have 'Christly' interaction is *not* suggesting the limp-wristed caricature of Jesus as an effete character floating around with a vacant smile and being 'nice' to everyone; rather, it is in the robust and incisive Jesus we see striding through the Gospels and modelling positive attitude and action, particularly among people who were 'other'. A prime example is that Jesus was consistently *for* the Samaritan immigrants of his day, in contrast to his colleagues, who behaved in a hostile manner or spoke badly of them.[18] Jesus did not appear to feel threatened by the presence of immigrants who were different in ethnicity, religion and identity from him, and who were marginalized by their culture or gender. Christly behaviour is radically different from a lot of the public discourse today.

There is a parallel between the experience of the Samaritans of Jesus' day and the British Muslims of our day. I am indebted to journalist and academic Jenny Taylor, who outlines the political journey of immigration to the UK.[19] She argues that, historically, Europe would not have known that it *was* Europe until Islam came along. She even suggests that the notion of a 'Christian Europe' can be traced back to the Battle of Tours in France in the eleventh century, after which Scandinavians were able to be baptized, but North African Muslims were not. We know that all cultures take their tone from their foundational religion (or lack of one) and this was true of Britain; that is, until its religious foundations were shaken around the turn of the twentieth century by Darwinian evolutionary theory, the two world wars, mass migration and the sexual revolution of the 1960s. The result was that Britons were no longer embracing Christianity as part of their social fabric, which caused a loss of former certainties that had provided the fixed moral core of the nation, even if people knew they were not living up to it. It is this malaise that leaves the continent of Europe open to people with deeper faith convictions than secular Britons.

Before the First World War, in 1901, the British Brothers' League was formed to oppose new immigration laws on the understanding that immigrants were a treacherous 'enemy within'. Fifty years later, in 1959, the White Defence League was formed with a similar belief, and then in 2010, fifty years after that, the English Defence League emerged. The post-war era became a period of intentional mass migration. The 1948 British Nationality Act aimed to speed up the rebuilding of the nation; this was followed in 1962 by the Commonwealth Immigration Act. Within two decades, between 2 and 3 million people were added to the UK population. A further twist in the tale is that in 2005, research by the Electoral Commission showed that among first-generation immigrants, 80% of black Britons and 50% of South Asian Britons voted Labour. The press quickly accused Labour of politicizing immigration to gain votes and intentionally try to break down the social class system and change Britain's cultural, ethnic and moral identity.[20] Successive governments (and the media) have tried to monitor the situation but have been hampered by their lack of 'religious literacy', which causes a clumsy handling of people of faith – including Christians.

Tribalism – 'Us' and 'Them'

The immigration journey in the UK nurtured an 'oil-and-water effect' which, although it is weakening, is still evident. In the early years, immigrant communities tended to cling for reassurance to one another and the cultural patterns they knew. For Muslims, this

included mosque attendance, observing feast days, wearing traditional dress, speaking their own languages, and enjoying online or
satellite TV access to news and views from their birth country. This
is something I witnessed among Brits living in the Middle East: they
would go to church, partly as a way of retaining a live link with their
own compatriots and culture via the festivals of the church calendar
and the embassy garden parties and community events. Some quietly
came to faith in Christ, which demonstrates an unrecognized sphere
of witness for active Christians living or working overseas.

In the early years of immigration to the UK, the British government was learning as things developed and could only respond to
what it saw; so, mistakes were made, such as the conflation of 'ethnicity' with 'religion' as if the two were the same thing. There was
also an expectation that all Muslim immigrants would become secu-
larized and integrate into the host culture, rather than enrich it with
their own.

As immigration continued, national disquiet was caused as the
government sought the advice of the so-called 'community leaders'
and individuals from groups such as the Muslim Council of Britain
(MCB). Unbeknown to the government, these included some hard-
line individuals with a social agenda to achieve a 'favoured community' status. This backfired when some local authorities lobbied
for special provisions for Muslim communities that other minority
groups were not getting.

Another unintended consequence emerged in areas such as Tower
Hamlets, London, where there was a predominance of Bangladeshi
Muslims, who would become over-represented on the local councils
to which they were duly elected. Some assertive Muslim councillors
began to obtain financial awards from the government's 'Prevent
Strategy' budget, which appeared to the public like paying Muslims
to create ghettos rather than integrate. This fuelled the negative narrative that Muslims had the local authorities under their thumb and
were aiming to take over by an incremental spread, known as the 'ink
blot' strategy, like ink on blotting paper which eventually merges into
total coverage – in other words, a takeover.

A survey by the local authority in Bradford described the situation as the creation of unintentional 'social apartheid', with 'no-go areas' in some parts of the country where South Asian enclaves existed.[21] Things were not going well, but it was *not* necessarily the fault of everyday Muslims, but rather the politicking that was going on over their heads and in their name, carried out by ambitious and articulate individuals and well-meaning civil servants too embarrassed to say no.

The word 'immigration' has become a political 'hot potato' in Europe, while for informed Muslims the word 'migrate' (*hijra* in Arabic) is a facet of Islamic belief; it carries the positive connotation of having a 'clean slate' by voluntarily abandoning what was and breaking ties with the old.[22] The closest parallel in Christian thinking might be the word 'pilgrimage'. However, for many indigenous white Britons, migration (for economic reasons or otherwise) is seen as a problem, particularly when it is unrestricted.

The Christendom instinct of 'territory' and the 'island nation' mentality surfaced sharply during the Brexit debate, particularly when it was thought that Turkey could possibly join the European Union, which would have enabled a further 83 million Turks to become eligible to enter the UK for work.[23]

Both secular and Christian media reflect conspiracy theories about immigration being an 'invasion' by stealth. Take, for example, the claim that the Gulf Arab states are conspiring with the Council of Europe to turn Europe into 'Eurabia'.[24] Evidence in a poll conducted by *Reader's Digest* shows that 79% of those questioned in the UK thought the number had been increasing over the two previous years, when it had actually fallen.[25] It was also thought that new migrants were a drain on the country, while figures showed that settled immigrants were contributing £2.5 billion into the economy – three times the cost of asylum seekers. Also, as the non-working population grows due to longer life expectancy, immigrants (of any description) will be increasingly needed, not just to meet the skills shortage but also to avert a national crisis in the growing pensions bill.

Sociologist Philip Jenkins says with specific regard to 'Muslim' immigration: 'The question is not so much how many Muslims there will be in Britain in 2050 but what kind of Islam they will espouse.' In contradiction to the press coverage of the lunatic fringe, the trend suggests they will espouse a 'Euro-Islam', as opposed to an 'Islamo-facism', because by 2050 the social attitudes and values of Muslims from immigrant families look set to broadly reflect those of 'old-stock' white Europeans. Jenkins adds the proviso that the number of Muslims who practise Islam is only a sizeable *fraction* of the total figure. I can vouch for this because British Muslims have told me that only about 20% are in mosque on a Friday. Jenkins reports that in France the figure is only 5%.[26]

In chapter 8 we will see that the fear of a Muslim takeover is a 'paper tiger' because many 'Muslims' (so called) are not actually practising Islam and would prefer to be identified as 'non-religious'; also, an unprecedented and growing number are identifying as 'ex-Muslim', with the biggest proportion of those becoming atheists, or 'Christ-followers' who are saying: 'Spiritually I follow Jesus, but culturally I have a Muslim background.' This is similar to a Jewish person who is openly non-religious or who has become a 'Messianic Jew' but who inevitably continues to see himself or herself as Jewish – ethnically if not culturally.

Strident Reaction to Radical Islam

For me, the biggest cause of strident attitudes towards Muslims/Islam is the behaviour of radical Muslims. As mentioned above, I am told anecdotally that only about 20% of British Muslims are in a mosque for Friday prayer. So, for the sake of argument, a personal guesstimate might be that if we rounded the figures, we might find that possibly two thirds of British Muslims tend towards the 'nominal' end of the spectrum (with some even 'non-religious') and that perhaps only a third are 'practising'.

Of those who are practising, we might find a further breakdown where two thirds are 'mainstream' (i.e. 'orthodox' or 'conservative') and a third might be classed as 'ultra-conservative'. Of this group, two thirds might be active in *dawah* (inviting others to Islam) whether socially or politically, and a third might be radical or even Islamist.

In my view, the negative narrative levelled at all Muslims is only accurate of this minority within a minority. This lunatic fringe is not content to merely '*join* the party' of life in the West; rather, their avowed aim is to take over the party and drag it back to the seventh century. This is their *jihad* or 'struggle', and they arrive at this mind-set because they *minor* on what mainstream Muslims major on, and *major* on what mainstream Muslims minor on.

To describe this sort of scenario another way:

- Most Muslims are guided by 'reason' (*'aql*), which I describe as the 'reasonable' or 'fair-minded' approach. They are usually as courteous as any other citizen and tend to see jihad not as 'holy war' on others but rather as a *personal* struggle where they strive for spiritual improvement in the same sense as the apostle Paul, who says: 'I strike a blow to my body and make it my slave so that after I have preached to others, I myself will not be disqualified for the prize' (1 Cor. 9:27).

- Some Muslims engage in propagation (*tabligh*) and can be characterized by words such as 'activist', 'outreaching' and 'defending' Islam by staffing book tables, and possibly debating. For them, jihad is about *dawah* (i.e. extending an invitation to Islam), a struggle to see Islam flourish.

- A tiny minority of Muslims see jihad as a licence to violence that is referred to as *fatah* (Arabic for 'conquest', 'opening up' or Islamic 'expansion'). Such Muslims tend to be younger, rarely scholarly, socially disadvantaged, ultra-devout to the point of fanaticism, politically oriented, and radicalized by themselves or someone else. These people are like a 'self-styled thought police' who are threatening Muslim governments that collaborate with the West, as well as any Muslim scholar who dares to engage theologically with contemporary issues, not to mention advocating the extermination of apostates (ex-Muslims).

The Size of the Problem

That said, according to available government figures, it is estimated that out of the 3 million British Muslims, 3,500 are on the radar of the British security services as being linked to the *fatah* category,[27] and a further 25,000 are being watched as 'people of interest'.[28]

The strident narrative about Muslims claims not only that *all* Muslims are violent but also that Islam itself is *inherently* violent. My response to this claim is that, like Old Testament texts, Islamic texts have the *potential* to be used as justification for violence; however, regardless of how high or low the figures may be, if all Muslims are inherently violent, why are so *few* Muslims on the police watch list?

No one has ever suggested that the behaviour of the IRA (*all* ostensibly Catholic) is proof that Catholicism is inherently violent, nor that all Catholics are violent or members of the IRA. It seems to me that both the IRA and Islamists are violent for similar reasons, which includes individual *ideology*, a personal *choice*, the *circumstances* surrounding their journey, and the fact that the anger and grievance is rooted as much in the quest for *power* as it is in religious conviction. That said, let us list some reasons why some Muslims abandon a 'mainstream' understanding and start interpreting religious texts as a mandate for violence:

- They may have a political agenda and use the banner of an ideology to achieve it.
- They may be idealists who believe that making the world a *sacred* place is a 'just cause'.
- Some Muslims are disengaged and caught between a host culture and the notion of a non-terrestrial Islamic State, which leaves them rootless and searching.[29]
- People who are vulnerable and susceptible can be groomed and then brainwashed.
- They may be psychopathic criminals who enjoy a James Bond style licence to kill.

- Some have mental issues or may even be demonically driven or infested.
- They are selective in their use of holy texts, choosing verses that validate their actions and ignoring others that do not.

The Strident Use of Sacred Texts

Like fundamentalist Christians or Hindus, radical Muslims tend to develop an ideology as a reaction to a social context. This is often done by the selective use of their holy texts to validate their attitude and actions. The Islamist world view emerged amid a cluster of social conditions, including the independence of former British protectorates which then became Islamic states, the Middle Eastern oil boom, and the formation of national alliances, which all contributed to a resurgence of Islamic confidence and assertiveness. In his book *Passionate Believing*,[30] Bishop Bill Musk examines fully the theological drivers, so suffice it to say here that the sacred texts of the three 'Abrahamic' faiths include the Jewish Tanakh (i.e. the Old Testament), the Christian Bible, and the Muslim Qur'an with Hadith writings. All of them are ancient in their world view and therefore contain references to violent actions, which would be understood in their historic context but which are now constrained by modern standards of international human rights. This does not stop those on the violent fringe of Islam, any more than it has stopped those on the violent Christian fringe, such as Timothy McVeigh (the 1995 Oklahoma bomber in the USA) or Anders Breivik (who in 2011 shot sixty-nine young people in Norway).[31] We may claim that such people are not *really* 'Christian'; if so, we need to extend the same courtesy to the violent fringe who claim to be 'Muslim'.

I have no figure for the number of violent texts in the Old Testament of the Bible, but there are over 200 such texts in the Qur'an. The problem is that the text is seen as *fixed* and therefore unable to be reapplied in the modern context; a problem that is avoided in Christian theology due to the interpretative disciplines of *exegesis* (the determining of the original meaning) and *hermeneutics* (the application of that meaning for today).[32] This process starts with the *natural* or obvious meaning of the text, which is not always literal. Sometimes a verse is highly context-specific and therefore a one-off that is restricted to its historic era, while other verses may be figurative. Some texts merely report violent events and do not necessarily endorse them. As a result of the process of applying ancient biblical texts to the present day, Christians no longer practise animal sacrifice (Lev. 9:3–4), or execute their adolescent children for going off the rails (Deut. 21:18–21), or stone people to death for adultery (Lev. 20:10), or undergo ritual circumcision (Lev. 12:3), or observe dietary laws (Lev. 11:1–47), or engage in the genocide of their enemies (1 Sam. 15:3).

The plot of the Bible is also developmental, or an unfolding narrative – the record of God's journey with humankind, which has passed through two eras: *before* Christ and *after* Christ. The age before Christ is captured in the Old Testament, which is the old 'arrangement' (i.e. the old covenant or testament). It is characterized by 'law', which served as a scaffold throughout history until the new 'arrangement' (the new covenant or testament), which is characterized by 'grace'. These two eras are inseparable and can only be understood in relation to each other, which is why Christians use *both* Old and New Testaments, particularly when interpreting the 'hard texts' – an option that does not exist in Islam because the Qur'an is an Old Testament document with no New Testament to assist it. The veteran commentator Amir Taheri identifies this as having a major impact on the Islamic tradition from its inception. He goes so far as to say that it has been causing a slow decline ever since the twelfth century. As a result, most Muslim clerics today find themselves ruling on matters of ritual detail or family life, while struggling to keep up with the broader challenges of a fast-changing modern world. The younger generation of Muslims are noticing that the text of the Qur'an (like the Torah) is *fixed*. Consequently, Islamic theology lacks the exegetical tools to develop a 'living theology', which not only restricts Muslim clerics but also forces them into the role of a 'curator' of the details of the Qur'an and Hadith, while being unable to account for the contemporary issues which are part of the felt need of Muslims in the modern world. Taheri sees this scenario as a 'crisis of legitimacy'.

However, Taheri advises non-Muslims *not* to draw a direct line between the historic Islamic texts and the current behaviour of radicalized Muslims[33] because the Islamist vision is rooted, less in the *content* of the text itself, and more in the panic that a modern application of the sacred text will rob Islamists of the *control* they crave. They engage in aggressive online propaganda as 'laptop jihadis'. Their goal is to try to stop modernization by seeking to lead Muslims *backwards* to the perceived 'glory days' of seventh-century Arabia.

The Strident Use of Statistics

Neither the media nor academia nor government are exactly bastions of 'religious literacy', yet their role in public discourse requires a discerning use of statistics about issues of faith. It is little wonder that the media is a main driver of the negative narrative about Muslims/Islam.

Gathering data about ethnic and religious minorities is always a delicate issue, partly because people from corporate cultures value 'saving face' as part of the honour/shame code, which can prompt the telling of 'white lies'. Any data is only as good as the method used to obtain it and the accuracy of the answers given. Data is only as good as it is reliable, and it is important to know whether something is a blip or a trend and how far it is a fair indicator of the future. This is important because statistics can become weaponized by people who use them to support a particular agenda.

For me, the most elusive voice to access is that of the 'silent majority' of British Muslims. Because I grew up in an immigrant family environment, when I was associating with people in a local church my father said to me: 'You seem to think you are white?' This opened the way for Muslim friends to tell me they felt they were merely born into a Muslim family but were not *religious*; rather, they felt duty-bound to keep up appearances as part of the cultural bond with their elders.

This delicate area was probed by the Pew Research Center in 2017, when researchers asked Muslims across Europe and North America how concerned they were about violence committed in the name of Islam. They found that 79% said they were 'somewhat' to 'very' concerned, while 21% said they were 'less' to 'not at all' concerned.[34] A similar survey asked if Muslim respondents sympathized or condemned Muslims who are involved in stoning women to death for adultery (a punishment still practised in a handful of Muslim states); in response, 79% condemned it (i.e. 66% 'completely' and 13% 'to some extent'). Such values were particularly true of the younger generations, who tend to resent being thought of as having the same opinions as their grandparents' generation when people tended to be less-educated rural villagers. Neither do such youngsters want to be tarred with the same brush as bigoted Islamists. Such views seem to tally with the notional 80/20 percentage split mentioned earlier.

Another survey in 2010 used methodology that managed to avoid the usual pitfalls and revealed that 8 out of 10 British Muslims say they 'feel British . . . if people would let them' and that their concerns were not that different from those of many non-Muslim counterparts on issues such as family life, their children's future, economic security, and the freedom to choose to practise faith, rather than being dictated to (as was the case in some of their countries of origin).[35]

Stridency and Temperament

Finally, why is it that two people, from a similar background, can read the same statistics and it has such a different impact on them? One can have a strident *reaction* while the other has a conciliatory *response*. For example, for every person who has said to me: 'Muslims really look after their elderly relatives better than us', someone else has said something like: 'The only language *they* seem to understand is military force.' One American Christian leader went public to call for the Qur'an to be publicly burned;[36] another US church leader put a sign outside his church urging people to flush the Qur'an down the toilet.[37] Such people seem unaware that their actions have consequences: when their words were picked up online in Kashmir, a Christian school was burned down, and innocent Muslims and Christians were killed in rioting.

When I saw one of these pastors interviewed, he was no 'shrinking violet', which leads me to suspect he filters available information in accordance with his temperament and personality type, which is more comfortable with 'binary thinking' (i.e. something is either good or bad, either black or white).

In my seminar work, I have occasionally seen active Christians walk out in disgust at the alternative facts being presented, which challenge their perception of Islam and Muslims, yet others have sat and quietly wept as they received the same information. Strident individuals tend to have a mental file labelled 'threat', and this file is often bulging with negative material received from news media, social media, certain Christian publications, maverick public speakers, some church pulpits, and even well-meaning mission workers who bring gloomy reports (perhaps as a subconscious 'pitch' for continued prayer and financial support). I find it a joy to watch people intentionally opening a new mental file labelled 'opportunity' or 'green shoots' or 'hope'. This is totally possible with the right balance of information.

The academic Tariq Modood suggests that the antidote to the negative narrative about Muslims/Islam is to ask some basic questions about civility, such as the following:[38]

1. Does the information stereotype Muslims by assuming they are all the same?
2. Is the information *about* Muslims or urging engagement *with* them?
3. Is the information facilitating mutual learning?
4. Is the language civil and appropriate to the context?
5. Is it criticism with an ulterior motive?

Such questions seem entirely reasonable and they are the sort of consideration which non-Muslims and Muslims alike do well to follow

as a 'benchmark' to aspire to. Such civility is simply positive PC etiquette, and it is urgently needed for interaction among Christians,
among Muslims as well as *between* Christians and Muslims.

This is a sobering fact, in light of the principle: 'a house divided
against itself cannot stand' (see Mark 3:25; Luke 11:17). My heart
goes out to Muslims who are starting to notice that the 'house of
Islam' is now showing serious signs of structural tensions that could
seriously damage its health, in the same way that stress can lead to a
heart attack. The medical expression for any obstruction is an 'occlusion', which is why I am calling this scenario 'Mount Occlusion' – the
next mountain blockage that could affect us all in different ways.

8

Mount Occlusion

Faith that is unreformed or progressive, and the phenomenon of defection

> The house of Islam is increasingly under pressure . . . and showing signs of a future implosion, due to the intellectual civil war going on over the issue of modernity and what to do about it.
>
> A. Taheri[1]

In this chapter we look at the arterial blockages within the house of Islam, asking why this is happening and how it is impacting the everyday Muslims who are abandoning unreformed Islam in increasing numbers to become secular, or atheist, or followers of Jesus Christ. We see how this is provoking reaction from traditionalists and hardline Muslims, and how both the desertion of faith and the repercussions confound PC rules.

An 'occlusion' is a medical term that refers to an internal stricture which could threaten the blood supply to the vital organs of the body, particularly the heart where it could cause that muscle to convulse in a heart attack and bring potential long-term debilitation. This scenario can reasonably be used to describe a global phenomenon that is happening to two major religious groups on the planet: first the largest one, which is Christianity; and second, the next largest one, which is the 'house of Islam'.

Occlusions in World Christianity

I must frame this chapter by starting with the Christian 'occlusions' which are threatening the well-being of Christianity, at least in its Protestant evangelical expression. This has come in the form of a 'prosperity gospel', which has travelled from the West to impact many churches of Africa and other parts of the Global South. Its roots are in North America, where the 'Word of Faith' theology managed to baptize the American dream of wealth and success to produce something like the Protestant work ethic on steroids, except that the 'hard work' part was replaced by faith. This aberrant expression of biblical Christianity has spread right around the English-speaking West.

A further stricture in western evangelicalism, particularly in the USA, is the practice of reading the Bible with an underlying addiction to 'certainty'. It has created a world view that has turned the Bible into a right-wing political manifesto, and as a result, the Southern Baptist Convention recently reported a loss of 200,000 members in one year. This defection is particularly true of younger generations, who have become 'de-churched' and are gravitating to issues around social justice and humanitarian causes; they find these to be a more congruent expression of their faith and the values of the kingdom of God.[2] The serious decline of formal Christian affiliation across the continent of Europe (and in the UK) is also public knowledge. With such defection going on among Christians, there can be no room for triumphalism when we compare it to a similar trend that is threatening the house of Islam.

Occlusions in the House of Islam

The popular perception is that Islam is the *fastest*-growing religion on earth, but this may not stand up to scrutiny, because the claim is based not on growth achieved through spectacular conversion rates but on the high birth rates in some Muslim populations. The evidence suggests that Islam may now be the fastest-*shrinking* religion on earth, because the number of *practising* adherents has dropped, signs of nominalism have increased, and the biggest defection in Islamic history is taking place. Why is this happening? What impact is it having on the 'house of Islam' and how is it affecting Christian/Muslim interaction, particularly in the West?

Which Will It Be: Mecca or Medina?

When I lived in the Middle East, I heard a lecture by the respected scholar of Islam, Bishop Kenneth Cragg. He spoke about a fork in the road for the religion, as competing 'priorities' emerged. The first was the *Meccan priority*, which refers to the early part of Muhammad's career in Mecca where his followers were a minority group living under pressure in a resistant atmosphere. The fledgling group was forced out, and the *hijra* journey was made, like an exodus, from Mecca to Medina, 270 miles to the north. This is where the *Medinan priority* started, and that location was the base for the latter part of Muhammad's career. In Medina, the fledgling Muslim community was protected, grew, and developed political influence through Muhammad, who was made governor of the city.

The chapters of the Qur'an which are attributed to the Meccan era are more reflective and have concerns that are more 'spiritual', including ethical issues similar to those that had been taken up by the minor prophets of the Old Testament, such as the needs of widows, orphans and the poor. The chapters attributed to the Medinan period contrast markedly with the Meccan ones. These are more political, abrasive, polemic, and intolerant of opposition. Some argue that if Meccan Islam serves Muslims when they are in a *minority*, Medinan Islam serves Muslims when they exist as a *majority* and are in control. Whatever the truth of that might be, this tension has played out in various ways throughout Islamic history and is very much in evidence today when the Medinan priority has in many respects become the modern Islamist ideology.

Islam in the Postmodern World

The question is: which 'priority' will Islam ultimately be defined by? Will it be the more 'spiritual' *Meccan* expression (i.e. a 'Euro-Islam') or will it be the aggressive, *Medinan* expression (i.e. 'Islamo-facism') of ISIS in Syria and Iraq, Al-Qaeda in Afghanistan, and Boko Haram in Nigeria? This tension has simmered under the surface for centuries and has been dubbed by some as the 'battle for the soul of Islam'.

What was triggered on 9/11 looks set to rumble on well into the twenty-first century, which may become the grand finale century that determines both the *future* and the *nature* of modern Islam.

My own life has been touched on several occasions by Islamist violence, for example when I experienced the impact of the demonic brutality unleashed in South Sudan, where the organization I worked with was supporting Christian and Muslim victims in a war zone. It happened again for me when an Iraqi ex-Muslim man I was helping was denied asylum in the UK and was repatriated to Iraq, where I linked him up with local Christ-followers via a cloak-and-dagger process. Sadly, his faith became known and he was shot dead within a week. It happened to me yet again when a Sudanese Christian woman, a friend of mine, was supporting her Muslim friend, having given her a Bible through which she became a Christ-follower. The new believer was found reading it, and this led to her being stabbed to death. I have also known others in Egypt, Pakistan, Afghanistan and Iran, from both Muslim and Christian backgrounds, who have been shot, stabbed, beaten to death or blown to pieces for what they represented as followers of Christ in 'Muslim territory'. I remember Afghani Muslims coming to the widow of a Christian development worker and apologizing for the extremists who had murdered her husband. I have also had some tense conversations with active western Christians who feel that the 'dark' behaviour of extremists should *not* be addressed by Christians. In my view, fair-minded people should stand in solidarity with one another across 'party lines'.

I love sincere Muslims and ex-Muslims everywhere, which compels me to speak up on their behalf to say that the violence and repression perpetrated against Muslims, by Islamist Muslims, is one of the biggest threats to the house of Islam today. It is driving their fellow Muslims out into the cold of atheism or else into the warmth of the arms of Jesus Christ.

Take, for instance, a woman I know from a devout Muslim family in the Horn of Africa who relates to the litany above. She shared how she became a Christ-follower after her friend sent her a link to a YouTube video clip of ISIS fighters executing an American hostage by decapitation. She was traumatized and unable to reconcile how anyone claiming to be 'Muslim' could behave in such a demonic way towards a fellow human being. She became deeply confused and angry with God, which prompted a re-evaluation of the religion of her birth. Eventually she concluded that she wanted nothing more to do with Islam. This led to a journey that ended in a heart allegiance to Jesus Christ, as a reaction to the 'Medinan priority' within the house of Islam.

I also met a western woman in Turkey whose language tutor was using Turkish daily newspapers for conversation practice. The headlines about jihadi violence kept coming up until one day the female tutor stopped the conversation and said: 'If this is the purest expression of Islam, I don't want to be a Muslim any more and I'll take off my *hijab* [headscarf].' I am constantly hearing such stories, particularly in testimonials given by such individuals on social media.

It seems to me that, all over the world, Muslim people are either making a conscious shift towards the more benign 'Meccan priority', or else voting with their feet and leaving the house of Islam altogether. The popular perception is that no Muslims are calling for change, but this is not true.

Dissenting Voices

A notable development in the movement for change are the progressive Muslim voices of people such as Maajid Nawaz, who is a former political Islamist with the group called Hizb-ut-Tahrir (now banned in the UK). Nawaz relented and turned progressive, arguing that Islamism and 'jihadism' are both 'innovation' (an Islamic term meaning not authentic and therefore unorthodox). He says that, apart from two occasions in Islamic history, no Muslim government has ever tried to enforce Islam on the whole of a society, opting instead for a *millet* system, whereby civil and religious laws were held as a dual authority, rather than the concept of an imposed theocracy which the extremists envisage today.[3]

The notion of Islamism is not essentially religious but *ideological*, and is found in the extremes of both major branches of Islam: Sunni (as in Saudi Arabian Wahhabism) and Shia (as in Iran). While these two branches have some distinctively different doctrines, they are based on the same holy texts of Islam and tend to major on material from the Medinan priority; both wish to usher in a new Islamic empire (i.e. caliphate) by exporting their respective robust versions of Islam. This is why the governments of Saudi Arabia and Iran have been known to finance the global Islamist franchises that have sprung up, such as ISIS or *Da'esh* (*Al-Dawlat al-Islamiyah fi al-Iraq wi ash-Sham*) (in Iraq/Syria), Al-Shebab (in North Africa, East Africa, and the Horn), the Aden-Abyan Islamic Army (in Yemen), the Taliban (in Afghanistan), Al-Qaeda (in Pakistan, Middle East and North Africa), and Boko Haram (in Nigeria). These governments have been found to conduct 'war by proxy' in countries such as Yemen and Libya, using autonomous groups to carry out violent attacks. It does not take a crystal ball to predict that, one day, we are likely to see the Sunni/Shia competitiveness escalate into an all-out conflict that would play out like a heart attack – the threat of Mount Occlusion.

Islamist ideology is 'ultra-conservative' and is effectively intent on taking Islam back to the perceived 'glory days' of the Early Middle Ages. When you get closer to this type of radical belief, it feels like *Pharisaism* on steroids, something Saul of Tarsus would have related to as he inflicted suffering and even death on those who had left Judaism to follow Jesus. Saul affirmed violence in the name of God (Acts 8:1; 9:1–2) and with the same religious zeal that I see inspiring Islamists today. Islamists accentuate the harsher aspects of sharia law, taking the letter of the law to its logical conclusion, which leads to human rights violations and anachronistic views that are barbaric and look absurd in the modern world.

Going back to the generational issue for a moment, I have sat with young professional Muslims who mock YouTube clips of leading clerics who say things such as: 'Women should not drive because it damages their ovaries', or 'The moon landing could not have happened because the Qur'an doesn't mention it'. The respected Muslim scholar Mona Siddiqui helpfully suggests here that this problem started four centuries ago when the Muslim world failed to participate with the West in the construction of modernity.[4] As a result, some Muslim nations were marginalized and even resentful about a sense of exclusion while the West flourished economically, albeit to the point of hegemony (as seen in chapter 4).

We have heard the analyst Amir Taheri speak about the inability of Islamism to offer a coherent response to the modern world, apart from seeking its demise. This is because it has an inadequate theology and no 'political programme' that can deal with modernity, which is why Islamism is losing ground to traditional and secular Muslim views. Taheri therefore sees Islamism as a 'mortally wounded beast' that has lost most major debates about modern life and Islamic political, economic, and social practice. Taheri refers to the academic Murad Ahmed who cites a poll by Policy Exchange in 2007, which found that almost a third of young Muslims said they would like to live under sharia.[5] When Taheri asks such youngsters to explain what sharia means, he finds they cannot. When he goes on to ask what they are really upset about in society, he says they seem to be 'born angry and looking for a reason for it.' Taheri therefore sees radical Islamism as an 'off-the-peg' solution that young Muslims can use to rebel against their parents and wider society, but that it is something many simply grow out of.[6]

Taheri goes on to say that in some mosques, God receives only a scant guest-mention in the Friday sermon in favour of obsessing about 'Zionist conspiracies', Islamophobia, the moral bankruptcy of western societies, and the American imposition of hegemony in the

world. This is causing a drift away from the core raison d'être of Islam
and is thought to be unsustainable, because politicized religion cheap-
ens the faith and denies adherents the succour it is meant to bring
them. It all makes no sense, but hardliners cannot see the unintended
consequence of their bullying, namely that they are unwittingly contributing to the very reform process they are against by cowering in
the face of the perceived moral superiority of 'nutcases' because they
seem to believe the faith more than others.

It is fair to say that some sort of 'reformation' is under way
within the house of Islam, the significance of which could prove to
be as significant as Protestantism was in Europe in the seventeenth
century. The old order is becoming part of the 'occlusion', as progressives press for change. My concern is for sincere Muslims who
are pained by signs of the disintegration that is going on. A united
front would help, but, like Christianity which has an estimated
30,000 denominations, part of the legacy of Muhammad is his
statement that the Islamic Ummah would split into seventy-three
factions with only one of them surviving – without saying which
and why.[7] This adds more context to the Sunni/Shia tension cited
above, but there are other tensions around theology and the status
of the religious texts.

Discoveries about Islamic History and Texts

Amr Shalakany is a Harvard-educated Carnegie scholar and one-time
Assistant Professor of Law at Cairo University. His research into sharia
law shows that the idea of an *unbroken* continuity throughout history
is not accurate because the very definition of sharia has changed over
time, as influences came into it from religious hardliners and even
non-Muslim thinking. Apparently, this has always been the case in
Islamic jurisprudence, but it has intensified over the past two centuries as sharia law has been crafted to serve the political agendas of
those who administer it.[8]

In 2008 a team at Ankara University's School of Islamic Theology undertook a controversial research project for the Department of Religious Affairs. The aim was to rediscover the 'original spirit of Islam' via *hadith* (sayings of Muhammad). They found that, over time, a growing proportion of these texts have been rendered obsolete, such as the 'law of apostasy', which was originally devised at a time when the fledgling community needed protecting from desertion if it was to survive; hence the death penalty was given for apostasy as if it were a form of treason, which is an anachronism today.

Another example is the rule that women should not be permitted to travel without a male chaperone. This was written at a time when travel was not safe, and so it may have been a protective measure for women. However, those who want to perpetuate a male-dominated culture obscure the fact that Muhammad himself said, on another occasion, that he 'longed for the day when a woman might travel long distances alone'. This too is redundant in the modern world. Other examples include 'honour punishments' and female genital mutilation (FGM), which are not in the hadiths and are illegal in western law. As a result of the Turkish research, a programme was set up to train 450 women as imams (i.e. *vaizes*) in a refreshed expression of Turkish Islam. No further update seems to be available on this project, but a spokesperson at the time said: 'This work changes the religion from being rules that must be obeyed, to one designed to serve the needs of people in a modern secular society. This is akin to the Christian Reformation. Not the same, but . . . something that is changing the theological foundations of Islam.'[9]

The *official* version of the Qur'an is thought to date back to the seventh century when the caliph Uthman ibn Affan (583–656) closed the canon and had all other versions destroyed. This 'authorized' version has therefore been thought by Muslims to be the *verbatim* word of God that has been miraculously and pristinely preserved down the centuries. However, as Muslim scholars are being exposed to modern scholarship, they are faced with the fact that the transmission of the text (*hifdh*) has 'holes' in it.

The hard-line Muslim propagator Mohammed Hijab took up this issue in an interview with the well-known Islamic scholar Sheikh Dr Yasir Qadhi, who went on the record to say:[10]

1. The doctrine of the perfect preservation of the Qur'an has holes in it and does not stand up to academic scrutiny.
2. Islam was gradually constructed over several centuries.
3. These facts have now come into the public domain via social media.
4. There are over thirty different versions of the Arabic Qur'an in circulation, and each one has differing 'diacritical markers' (i.e. vowels, dots and grammatical symbols), some of which change words and meanings.
5. This should not be discussed in public nor by the uninitiated because it requires a 'deep dive into issues that are awkward and difficult'.
6. He (Qadhi) had hit the problem while studying Islamics at Yale University, prompting a 'crisis of knowledge'.
7. Muslims who question Islamic texts hit a 'red line' and are forbidden to go further, accepting this restriction by faith.
8. The *ulema* (top scholars) in the Muslim world are unaware of what western scholars have found and would be unable to answer their questions satisfactorily.
9. Muslims should accept in good faith that all thirty versions of the Qur'an are *perfectly* preserved and are the verbatim word of God – ignoring all contradictions.
10. He knows a dozen Muslim academics who have had a major crisis of faith over this issue and thinks one of them has left Islam.

Qadhi went on to describe the traditional position on textual preservation as 'simplistic', 'standardized', 'triumphalistic' and 'ossified'. He also spoke of 'an ever-growing group of intellectually curious Muslims who will find the standard narrative holds little academic weight' and concluded that 'a rational mind simply cannot acknowledge [the official Muslim position] as true'.

A Crisis Is Brewing

I feel for those caught up in this unfolding crisis because, in a globalized and online world, these findings cannot be hidden. On 10 January 2020, the Saudi journalist Ahmad Hisham wrote an online article called 'Amending the Qur'an', which was posted on the Saudi website Saudi Opinions (www.saudiopinions.org). It called for the textual errors in the Quran to be re-examined in the light of 'modern perceptions'. Then in July 2020 the Kurdish Iraqi journalist and political analyst Jarjis Gulizada wrote an article entitled 'A Call for Rewriting the Qur'an'. This was for *The Elaph* (www.elaphmorocco. com), an online newspaper that demanded an overwrite of the Qur'an as well as a re-examination of the principles of sharia law. Both articles point out the existence of 2,500 textual errors in the text, including syntax, spelling, grammar, and issues related to 'modern perceptions', which one assumes are violations of international human rights. The claim that the Qur'an needs 'correcting' is a contradiction of the belief in its perfect preservation, but it also appears to cast a shadow on the Islamic understanding of the divine inspiration of the Qur'an in the first place.[11]

Changing Status Quo

Another change agent is the end of the old monopoly of clergy and government bureaucrat influence as public education improves, which is why the Taliban are resistant to education, particularly of girls. Add to this the increasing numbers of Muslims who travel for university education or training and return as part of the growing urban middle class.

Then there is exposure to the rest of the world via social media, the internet, satellite TV and the film industry, which makes it impossible to shut out the effects of modernity. All of this fosters a more individual perspective on life, which has a knock-on effect in Muslim societies, which are *group*-oriented, with virtual connections between families in East and West to create a conduit for increased information, changing perceptions and new aspirations.

Taj Hargey is chair of the Muslim Educational Centre of Oxford, where he is also imam of the Summertown Islamic congregation. As an avowed *progressive* Muslim, he won a High Court libel case against a Muslim publication which had accused him of belonging to a 'heterodox' sect and thereby being a 'heretic' who should be excommunicated. He hopes his victory will embolden other progressives to challenge what he refers to as the 'self-appointed community leaders' who conduct witch-hunts to protect their power. He sees them as custodians of a 'warped' and 'backward-looking manifestation of the [Islamic] faith', which is 'foreign' (i.e. Saudi Arabian). He criticizes the South Asians who copy Arab dress codes – men growing untrimmed beards and women wearing the *niqab* (full-face veil with slits for the eyes). He says Saudi Arabia only has this influence due to its role as curator of the holy sites and its massive petrodollar wealth with which to entice Muslims via financial support. For Hargey, all thinking Muslims must resist and save 'British Islam' from foreign-inspired zealots.[12]

We have already mentioned the former radical Maajid Nawaz who has turned progressive and set up the Quilliam Foundation, a London-based think tank, challenging the premise behind Islamic extremism, and lobbying government and public institutions for more nuanced policies regarding Islam, greater democracy in the Muslim world, and the empowering of the 'moderate' Muslim voice. Nawaz says the public only hears those who 'pretend' to speak for all British Muslims, of whom he suggests only 25% look to the Muslim Council of Britain (MCB) for leadership.[13] Such community leaders are not always educated and can be less engaged in wider society, and therefore not necessarily qualified to speak for others. They are also not easy to hold to account, especially when they are aided and abetted by negative political correctness, which is weaponized to protect them and serve their agenda. I notice that politicians do not go to the vicar of a local parish church to get the views of the people who live in the parish, many of whom do not even attend church, yet this has been the approach in some Muslim communities with regard to the imams.

Melanie Phillips is a prominent reporter of these issues who took the view that if the UK were to continue on its trajectory, it would pose an existential threat to the British way of life, unless the voice of everyday Muslims can be heard. In 2006 Phillips wrote the book *Londonistan*, warning of the danger that the UK has been a 'soft touch' and a haven for Islamists.[14] Although for some her argument appeared overstated (even alarmist), it would seem there was an element of truth to it, judging by the fact that the seeds being sown came to fruition in the shape of the ongoing Islamist attacks in London since then. Whatever our view on this, the security services do appear to have 'upped their game'.

An aspect not picked up by Melanie Phillips has been added by the TV journalist Rageh Omaar, who points out that the gravitation to London among Muslim activists was not all bad or sinister. Quite the reverse, because at the same time as the advent of the 'dangerous religionists', the instability across the Muslim world has also caused Muslim media, Muslim publishers, Muslim free-thinkers and dissidents alike to base themselves in London because it is freer and safer in the UK. The West is becoming part of the reforming story that is quietly influencing the future of theology, politics and identity in the house of Islam.

Green Shoots of Reformation

The academic Tariq Ramadan affirms the neutrality of the western setting, saying that in the West it is easier for many Muslims to practise their Islam in accord with their conscience than it is in some Islamic states.[15] A person I met and should be noted in this context is Ghayasuddin Siddiqui, a founder of British Muslims for Secular Democracy.[16] I am reliably informed that he and a relative are part of 'City Circle', an open discussion forum for young Muslims on the Edgware Road in London, where they celebrate good news stories of shared community projects. They are weary of the bad news and want more than platitudes about interfaith dialogue. There is also a Bradford-based initiative called the Muslim Women's Council, which is active in fundraising to establish what could become the first women's-led mosque in the UK.[17]

The Birmingham-based Muslim Women's Network exists to see Muslim women protected from the potential for unfair treatment under sharia law in nineteen countries. Its members are campaigning to get Muslim women to register their marriages with the state as a precaution against arbitrary divorce or desertion. An allied project is the Register Our Marriage campaign led by Aina Khan, which is active in Bradford and elsewhere.[18]

Another example is Abdul-Azim Ahmed of the Muslim Council of Wales, who has worked with Christians to set up a religious freedom initiative, and his colleague, the Islamic scholar Dr Usama Hasan, who openly supports the repealing of the 'apostasy law'; he calls for an internal discussion within Islam on the issue. The website Apostasy and Islam (www.apostasyandislam.blogspot.co.uk) was set up in 2007 by progressive Muslims to create another voice within Islam calling for the religious freedom they believe the Qur'an endorses.[19]

There is also a growing number of writers (male and female) who are either progressive Muslims or who have become 'ex-Muslims'. Among their number are social activists such as Wafa Sultan, who said: 'I have no choice; I am questioning every single teaching of our holy book.'[20] She is joined by authors at the political level, such as lawyer and novelist Abda Khan,[21] Irshad Manji[22] and Ayaan Hirsi Ali.[23] Others are writing at a more academic level, including Ali Abd al-Raziq[24] and Abdel Wahab El-Affendi.[25] At the theological level are scholars such as Sheikh Ali Gomaa,[26] and also Abdullahi Ahmed An-Na'im[27] and Adnan Khan.[28] All such writers are propagating a form of Islam that accounts for contemporary realities, rather than assuming the world should change to fit in with it.

Millennial Muslims

The Millennial generation comprises people who are 40 years old or under, that is, those who came to adulthood around 2000. While we know that a tiny minority of this generation become radicalized, it is helpful to know that others go the opposite way. For example, one Millennial Muslim young man, whose parents came to the UK fifty years ago, said he had only ever spent a handful of months in Pakistan, yet since the attacks in New York on 11 September 2001, he has felt like a stranger in Britain due to people's suspicion of him. He admits being one of the non-religious or 'nominals' when he says: 'I'm not much of a Muslim as religion isn't a big part of my life.' We said earlier that members of this generation of Muslims are social media savvy and more aware of the wider world. They are less patient with the anachronistic pronouncements of senior clerics, whose teaching they may struggle to engage with.

Millennial Muslims are inevitably going to be ahead of the curve in their openness to voices such as Amir Taheri, when he says that apart from the leaders of a small group of hard-line Muslim countries, virtually all Muslims would acknowledge that fair elections are the best source of government legitimacy.[29] Younger academics too (especially females) are challenging misogyny and the archaic teaching of a male-dominated clergy who appear to be out of touch. Two world views are starting to collide as the emerging generations look for something more relevant to their lives in the modern world.

Muslims Online in a Global Village

I vividly remember standing in line at Kabul international airport in Afghanistan behind a short, bearded man in his thirties who was wearing the impressive tribal turban and local dress. I was tall enough to see over his shoulder and noticed he was cradling a large smartphone, which suddenly burst into life at high volume. He moved like lightning to turn it off because he had been in the middle of an online porn video – a reminder of how interconnected the globe is, though not always for the best reasons.

The word 'internet' is short for 'interconnected computer network'. In 1997 there were fifty online networks broadcasting in eleven languages around the clock. Iran had 6 million people accessing the internet daily, and 3.5 million viewing two Arabic satellite TV networks. By 2015 an estimated 413 million people in the Middle East and North Africa (MENA) had an internet connection. The level of penetration in each country was between 48% and 77%.[30]

Cyberspace, like political correctness, is a double-edged sword for good and ill. For example, wicked and pernicious material can flow online, serving the purposes of radical propaganda as well as enabling planning and secret communication among terrorists via the so-called 'dark web'. The flip side to this is that the internet also facilitates freedom of anonymous enquiry, virtual access to the world, and exposure to information. As a result, millions of Muslims are encountering the good news about Jesus Christ and significant numbers are choosing to follow him via virtual means. For instance, in the Middle East there is now a growing Me Too movement among women who are finding their voice together to bring male sexual abusers to justice.

Muslim Persecution of Muslims

A report by the US National Counterterrorism Center found that over the past five years, Muslims were seven times more likely than non-Muslims to be victims of Islamic violence.[31] Various other groups were targeted, such as political dissidents, gay individuals, or westerners, such as those at work in the office of the *Charlie Hebdo* magazine in Paris, or commuting in underground trains and buses in London, or at leisure in a nightclub in Bali, at entertainment venues such as the Bataclan in Paris, or at the Manchester Arena.

Christians and Jews also feature highly as targets, according to a landmark article by journalist John Allen, who claimed: 'the global persecution of Christians is the unreported catastrophe of our time.'[32] The Muslim persecution of Christian minorities is only part of it because the International Society for Human Rights found that 80% of global religious discrimination is directed at Christians. The Center for the Study of Global Christianity at Gordon Conwell Theological Seminary, Massachusetts, found that 100,000 Christians a year and

11 every hour are killed in a 'situation of witness'. Discrimination against Christians goes on in 139 countries according to the Pew Forum in 2019. Little wonder that the Christian Institute finds itself having to provide a legal defence for British Christians who are being discriminated against in the UK, partly due to the weaponizing of politically correct legislation.[33] The organization Open Doors says that out of the top 50 nations with the worst human rights record, 31 have Islamic governments[34] that tolerate (or even encourage) political and fanatical groups in acts of repression, which makes Christians the most persecuted group on the planet. This is a point that has caught the attention of politicians, and public figures such as the Prince of Wales, as well as church leaders. The silence from Islamic authorities on the issue is apparently a source of disillusionment to Muslims, who want to dissociate themselves from such injustice and abuse of human rights.

I first encountered this disillusionment for myself in the 1970s when my Persian friends in the UK told me about the Iranian government's sustained repression, intimidation, arrest, imprisonment, torture and martyrdom of political dissenters, including the murder of Christian leaders such as Haik Hovsepian Mehr. It is little wonder that so many Iranians have become disillusioned with the totalitarian brand of Islam behind such repression. The trickle of asylum seekers in the 1970s has been joined by those from several other Muslim countries to become the current stream, which is like a lava flow from a volcanic eruption, as people flee various parts of the Muslim world to seek sanctuary in 'Christian' countries.

Muslims Abandoning Islam

Over the past twenty years I have been meeting more and more Muslims who have changed their heart allegiance from Islam to Jesus Christ or to atheism. Some will inevitably be claiming a Christian faith to strengthen an asylum application, but many became Christ-followers in their birth countries, before having to flee for their lives.

The graph of the numbers of Muslim-background people leaving Islam shows a parallel curve with those of Jewish heritage who are turning to Jesus as the Messiah. The similar trajectory over the past three decades is striking.

Several factors are combining to create what is now the biggest movement of Muslims to Christ in history. Besheer Mohamed is a senior researcher at the Pew Center and says that 23% of Muslims in the USA have abandoned Islam.[35] The list of reasons includes:

1. the repression and persecution of Muslims by Islamists
2. the availability of Bible translations in Muslim languages
3. the material about Jesus in the Qur'an and online, acting as a stepping-stone to the Bible
4. having a Christian friend
5. experiencing dreams and visions
6. the global awakening among Christians worldwide to pray for Muslims, a trend which has emerged in tandem with the unprecedented numbers changing a Muslim heart allegiance to accept the claims of Christ
7. access to online enquiry and the availability of media such as satellite TV, radio, and social media platforms
8. exposure to academic scrutiny of the historic foundations of the Islamic tradition.

Muslim Leaders Respond

Muslim leaders are now starting to talk on YouTube about this phenomenon of defection from Islam. Ten scholars convened a conference in Canada on the issue of 'Atheism and Islam', and Imam Dr Bilal Philips spoke openly and pastorally at the Abu Huraira Center in Toronto about Muslims abandoning Islam (particularly those under 40 years old).[36] He confirms that young Muslims, in particular, are leaving Islam and that many are becoming non-religious (or even atheist). According to the testimony of 'ex-Muslims', the decision is so costly that some simply become 'uber-nominal', opting for a quiet life by retaining an external Muslim identity within their family and community, telling no one and becoming a 'closeted' ex-Muslim. Others are very upfront about their decision and set up their own social media pages, including revealing their face and identity.

In 2011 one informed analyst estimated that in many countries it is 'hundreds' leaving Islam, in others it is 'thousands', in at least four countries that he knows it is more like 'ten thousand', and in a further three countries it is probably over 'a hundred thousand'.[37] A researcher at the Centre for Migration Policy, Swansea University, estimated the figure in the UK to be around 50,000.[38] A journalist at the *Washington Times*, Joel Rosenberg, interviewed retired Iraqi general Gewargis Sada, who was security advisor to Jalal Talabani, the first president of Iraq after Saddam Hussein. Sada said that hundreds of Iraqi Muslims were turning to Christ around the time Saddam was toppled. He went on to say that the 'throne room' in the Baghdad presidential mansion was turned into an evangelical church. He reported: 'Kurds are especially receptive and converting to Christianity in their hundreds.' An estimated 5,000 Iraqi Muslims publicly identified as followers of Christ after the 'liberation of Iraq', and 8 out of 10 of them had done so because Jesus had appeared to them. The prime minister of the Kurdistan Region, Nechirvan Barzani, said: 'I would rather see a Muslim become a Christian than a radical Muslim.'[39] In an interview on Al-Jazeera TV, the Libyan cleric Sheikh Ahmad al-Katani said that 'in Africa alone about six million Muslims are leaving Islam every year'.[40]

'Non-Islamiosity'

Among the Christ-followers from Muslim backgrounds in Iran there is a concept called 'non-Islamiosity'.[41] This means to 'de-islamicize' one's life by leaving the Ummah (worldwide community of Muslims) and dropping the formal religious observances of Islam, while retaining the biblically affirmed or neutral aspects of one's family and

Islamic heritage and reorienting them into the way of Christ; in short, this is becoming a 'cultural Muslim'.

Ex-Muslims

Those who are leaving Islam now form a growing worldwide movement. Since its inception in 2010, the movement has established itself in sixteen countries, coordinated through a Central Council of Ex-Muslims. Before the movement came along, the popular perception was that to abandon Islam meant a person was an intellectual, such as the writer Ibn Warraq or Salman Rushdie. However, 'ex-Muslims' provides a category for people from all walks of life to fit into. Among the founding figures are women such as Mina Ahadi, who fled for her life from the Iranian regime in 1996; Maryam Namazie, an Iranian human rights campaigner; Pakistani-born Sara Raidar; and Egyptian political scientist Hamed Abdel-Samad.[42] The movement is a virtual connecting-point via internet chat rooms and social media platforms, where stories and views are shared openly by people willing to be seen.

Another development in this regard are some peaceful mass protests that have been gathering momentum in Iran, where women have been publishing online pictures of themselves without their head scarves on, and some are discarding them altogether. This protest has a Facebook page called My Stealthy Freedom, which has a million subscribers – numbers that are too big for the authorities to control.

Some ex-Muslims call themselves 'secular Muslims' because they want to identify 'culturally' with Islam but not 'religiously'. An example of this is a young barrister, Mohsin Zaidi,[43] who is from a Pakistani family and was shortlisted by the *Financial Times* as a future LGBT leader. His family eventually accepted and supported his coming out and engagement to marry a white non-Muslim man. The network of secular Muslims includes something called the 'Inclusive Mosques Initiative' and also British Muslims for Secular Democracy,[44] a not-for-profit organization dedicated to supporting secularism in the UK. The latter was founded in 2006 by Nasreen Rehman and the well-known journalist Yasmin Alibhai-Brown. The group believes that the diversity of views among British Muslims is not adequately understood or represented to wider British society and that the image of Muslims is therefore distorted.

Sadly, many ex-Muslims are facing four main accusations, which they speak freely about, including:

1. They did not dig deeply enough into Islam by studying the right Islamic scholars. The defectors' response is that some of them did precisely that, which is why they left.
2. They are seeking attention. The defectors say the attention is only ever negative and usually hostile, and that no one in their right mind would put themselves through that on a whim.
3. They are doing it for fame and money. The defectors argue there is no money to be made, and that the only people making any are the prominent Islamic propagators who earn serious money from oil-rich states.
4. They are trying to please white people. This accusation appears to come from a colonial and racist mindset.

The Scale of the Defection

The doctoral research of David Garrison made statistics available on the 'movements' of Muslims to Christ that are going on around the world. Garrison defines a 'movement' as either 100 new Christ-following communities (i.e. churches) being created or 1,000 baptisms recorded, both within a period of twenty years.[45] Given this benchmark, Garrison found such 'movements' in 70 locations in 29 Muslim nations spread across the entire 'spiritual empire', from West Africa to Indonesia. In some locations these movements are affecting tens of thousands, and the last published total estimate was between 2 million and 7 million Muslims who have changed their heart allegiance to Jesus Christ and have been baptized. This number is now known to be rising annually and has become unwise to publish.

Garrison's research shows that since the founding of Islam fourteen hundred years ago, there has been little movement of adherents away from it; that is, until the end of the twentieth century.

After the West came through the turbulence of two world wars and the great economic depression, social and political upheaval began in Iran, Algeria and Bangladesh and the Soviet Union disintegrated. Against this backdrop, Garrison identifies the addition of eleven new movements of Muslims to Christ. Garrison goes on to say:

> In the opening years of the 21st century, the monolith of Islamic resistance to the gospel begins to crumble. In just . . . 12 years . . . we can identify and document a surge of 69 additional movements of at least 1,000 Muslims coming to faith in Jesus Christ and believers' baptisms. Behind the veil of violence and conflict that so plagues the Muslim world, thousands of Muslims are walking away from Islam and placing their trust in Jesus as the Son of God and unique pathway to salvation.[46]

Eyewitness accounts are coming to light to report scenes that are reminiscent of the Acts of the Apostles, including imams becoming Christ-followers, and Christ-centred worshipping communities (churches) being set up; also, Muslims are having dramatic dreams, visions, miracles, healings and supernatural encounters, and there are repeated cases of entire mosques changing allegiance to Christ.[47]

Some Christian critics are cautious about these 'movements' and ask whether they are a genuine work of the Holy Spirit, or a 'Jesus sect' of Islam. In my view this suspicion may be influenced by Mount Imperial and Mount Hegemony. My sense is that the discomfort of some critics is based on the fact that such goings-on are happening without the involvement of external people (i.e. western missionaries). We must be cautious not to require these new believers to tick our western doctrinal boxes, but rather assess them against the New Testament pattern. The expectations of our own theological tribe will also be culturally biased about what 'good' looks like, so we need to try to understand what is happening on a case-by-case basis. If improvements could be made among these new communities of believers, surely that places an onus on us to come alongside and 'explain to [them] the way of God more adequately' (see Acts 18:26), rather than becoming armchair critics. Can we free ourselves from western *preferences* and ensure that we are being 'theological' and not just 'cultural' in our expectations? If we manage this, we may avoid the 'elder brother syndrome' (Luke 15:11; cf. 28–32), which is at the heart of my book *Gospel for Muslims*, where I say:

> The identity, dress, and patterns of worship [amid people movements to Christ] sometimes appear to be closer to a Christ-centred sect of Islam than they are to a 'Christian church'. Such people-movements to Christ are coming about without outside help; although they are in some sense 'beyond [institutional] Christianity', they are 'inside the kingdom of God' and 'under the leadership of the King'.[48]

As the slow 'occlusion' in the house of Islam develops and threatens its health, this issue is part of the backdrop to interaction between Muslims and Christians. Although we are seeing evidence to the contrary, can active Christians learn to approach the issue with empathy, knowing how they would feel if anything similar were to happen in world Christianity? Can we become active facilitators, supporting those who are trying to navigate their way through the mountains and over the rough ground to discover 'Grace Pass'?

To achieve this, there is one last mountain blockage which, if not navigated, is in danger of making many active Christians a part of the problem rather than a part of the solution. It is setting Christians at odds with their fellow Christians over issues such as what the Christian message is, what other faiths are in relation to Christianity, what best practice in faith conversation looks like, and whether there are aspects of the teaching of other faiths that can be affirmed biblically. Let us try to find some answers as we turn to the final mountain – Mount Mission.

9

Mount Mission

When we are less help and more hindrance, and the battle over interactive styles

There are known knowns. These are things we know
that we know. There are known unknowns. That is to
say there are things that we know we don't know. But
there are also unknown unknowns. There are things
we don't know we don't know.

Donald Rumsfeld[1]

In this chapter we see how the issues discussed in the other chapters
have had a cumulative effect by provoking conflicting views among
Christians about Muslims/Islam and what Christian witness should
look like. We examine the four major interactive 'styles', including
'conversation', 'dialogue', 'apologetics' and 'confrontation'. We define
and describe these styles, giving examples of good and bad practice
in each one. We analyse how they should complement rather than
compete with one another.

Mount Mission is a blockage that affects the faith interaction of active
Christians as much as it does for active Muslims. It is the cumulative
effect of the influence of the previous mountain blockages mentioned
so far. These seep into our perception of ourselves and of the other
participant in an interaction. Mount Mission seems to be at the heart
of public discourse because it raises big issues about the nature of a

'religion' and the lived experience of its adherents. For example, it asks:

- what *true* religion should look like (e.g. is it benignly spiritual, or vocally political, or radically ideological, or physically violent?)
- what an *authentic* 'Christian' or 'Muslim' is, when even their co-religionists do not agree
- what the respective Scriptures say is *permissible* and acceptable, when propagating their respective 'message' in public space
- what impact political correctness is having on religious propagation and expression in public space.

This chapter sets out the four most used styles of interaction, whether private or public, and why *all* of them are appropriate according to the context in which they are used. It also describes what *good* and *bad* practice looks like when we 'render to Caesar what is Caesar's' (i.e. when we are PC-compliant) or 'render to God what is God's' (i.e. are faithful to our respective messages).

All four of the styles we will examine are neutral in the sense that they are used in secular society as well as the faith-group sphere. The styles are equally applicable when addressing issues such as racism, the new atheism, populist nationalism, abortion, sexual minority issues, the clash of visions between fundamentalist Christians and Muslim (i.e. kingdom or caliphate?), or any other social 'hot potato', which inevitably makes all these issues 'political' to some degree.

While secular society may not see the need for much *restraint* in tone, other than what is now legally required to avoid prosecution for 'hate speech', faith groups such as Muslims and Christians are constrained (at least in theory) by the requirements of their respective Scriptures, which adjudicate what is acceptable in their attitude and actions towards others.

That said, human nature suffers from 'blind spots', which stop us seeing the impact we may be having on others due to an understanding of our holy text, which works its way out in our attitude and actions with people in our own tribe and those of another tribe. Donald Rumsfeld, the former US Secretary of Defense under President George W. Bush in 2001, oversaw the military engagement in Afghanistan that was part of the so-called 'War on Terror' following the attacks of 9/11. There were cross-cultural implications involved, which was unfamiliar territory, and this prompted Rumsfeld to notice that this had not been factored in by the American psyche at the time – it was a 'blind spot'. He went on to articulate that a blind spot is not just something we do not *know*, but also something we do not *realize* that we do not know. His statement was a call to us all for more humility, as we are all blinkered about the influence of imperialism, hegemony, PC and racism, which is feeding the current climate of stridency. All of us need to 'self-critique' more, not least those within western evangelicalism, with its addiction to *certainty* and the binary thinking we talked about earlier. I heard a leading American evangelical say: 'To be right but in the wrong way is to be wrong.' We must be convinced of our views, while seeking to avoid being oblivious to things that are *unknown unknowns* to us. We are all more prone to this when we only hear from others in our own social or political or theological silo of opinion. The net result of this among evangelical Christians has not only been to decline to affirm one another, but also to be unable to *collaborate* with each other on issues that are agreed on. This is the point where Christians become part of the blockage I am calling 'Mount Mission'.

Before we go further to look at the styles of interaction, let me paint a word picture of two friends of mine who interact with Muslim people but could not be more different from each other in their understanding of what they are doing and why. I have spoken in both of their local churches and am aware that the party line in each church is scepticism about the thinking and activities of the people in the other church, which is unfamiliar to them and even offends their sensibilities to the point where they dismiss that church as 'wrong' and find biblical justification for doing so, without first checking to see if they have a blind spot that has been triggered. Let me describe my two friends who reflect the outlook and ethos of their respective local church communities.

Christian 'A'

First, there is Lesley, a person I have spent quality time with. She is a Christian community worker in a highly multicultural area of Britain known as 'the Asian Corridor'. Lesley is part of a mainstream evangelical church which, instead of expecting Muslims to come from the community to their building (although some do come to special social events in the church hall), the leadership commissions Lesley to go out into the community. Over the years, Lesley has built up respect among the local Muslims as someone who is available to them, and this has earned her the right of access into the lives of extended families, where she is a trusted confidante. In this context, individuals discreetly ask Lesley for prayer and enquire about having a personal relationship with God through Jesus. People are also being nurtured in a faith in Christ. She is asked regularly to pray with people about complex family issues, including the need for physical healing or protection from demonic harassment within some households.

For Lesley, the Great Commission of Christ is primarily to '*make disciples* of all nations' (Matt. 28:19), which she sees as addressing an individual as a whole person, not because they are a Muslim and certainly without objectifying them as a representative of Islam. Her interactions are mostly with everyday Muslims who might not necessarily be proficient in their knowledge of Islam; nor seek to propagate it, let alone try to put Christianity down. If anything, they tend to see Lesley as a spiritual cousin who sticks with them as they try to live their lives amid social difficulties, not least that of being Muslim in the current social climate.

Any reference Lesley makes to the teachings of Islam are usually en route to conveying the message of Christ to a person's felt need, rather than to discuss Christian differences. Lesley is one of the most modest people I know as she seeks to *be* good news, rather than arguing *about* good news. She interacts in a bespoke way to each individual, which she sees as a cultural courtesy, as well as being more effective.

Christian 'B'

No one could be more different from Lesley in approach than my second friend, Frank. His local church is also a thriving evangelical church in a similar multicultural area. The church has a strongly conservative evangelical ethos and a track record of open-air preaching and literature distribution. Frank interacts with Muslim passers-by via a Christian book table in the local high street, where there is also an Islamic book table staffed by local Muslims whose mosque background and outlook parallels Frank's church and theological outlook. His faithful presence in this public space has helped develop links with the Muslims who alternate to staff their table.

These individuals are informed and confident Muslims, who are well motivated and even passionate about outreach, including engaging with Christians about the differences in the two faiths and their view that Islam makes Christianity redundant. Over the years, Frank has developed a level of cordiality with his Muslim counterparts, which is almost a sense of camaraderie between the two book table teams. They bring to one another's attention new publications, which leads to the critiquing of one another's resources. All this enables good-natured, if robust, arguments about Christian and Muslim teaching. Frank differs from Lesley because he takes the view that before an individual Muslim can consider the message of Christ, their allegiance to Islamic teaching needs to be looser to enable them to engage with the 'what if' of new information. Therefore, for Frank, interaction with a Muslim is only necessary with the avowed and open aim of lowering the psychological barrier of the other participant, which may be based on a false premise or on misinformation about

Christianity. He spends almost all his time interacting with young males who are radical in their thinking and highly motivated in their desire to put down other faiths, especially Christianity and Judaism.

Everything in the outlook of both Frank and his Muslim friends tells them that the conveying of their message is primarily about *verbal proclamation* (i.e. the articulation of what is *true* and defending it against what is perceived to be *false*). Frank sees this as the most effective way to interact with his more informed, motivated and assertive Muslim friends who are looking for a doctrine-based interaction. Perhaps the biggest difference between Frank and Lesley is that for Frank, anything that looks remotely like social engagement is suspected of being a 'social gospel', while for Lesley, Frank has a truncated or 'reductionist' understanding of what the gospel is.

Horses for Courses

If we were to put the members of Lesley and Frank's local churches in a room and ask them to explain to each other the rationale for their perspective, there might be some tension in the room, depending of course on how feisty people's temperaments were. If there was the sort of squabble I have often witnessed, both between churches and between individuals in the same church, my advice to them would be that it is not a case of *either/or* but *both/and*. Both Lesley and Frank are right, but only in their distinctive settings where they are interacting with Muslim individuals whose contexts are markedly different. They are also fulfilling complementary aspects of the Great Commission of Christ; so the bottom line is that their styles of interaction need each other. They are *not* in competition (or should not be).

We shall see shortly that Jesus modelled the inseparable blend of both *word* and *action*, which I call 'grace and truth' (John 1:14,17). Lesley's approach is *relational* and *whole life* in its engagement. It is the unspoken language of love, which models the good news about Jesus through 'good works' which serve as light in society (Matt. 5:16). Misunderstanding arises when we fail to see that words and action go together like the proverbial horse and carriage. The 'good works' accompany the 'good words'; random acts of 'grace' are the mood music for the lyrics of the gospel.

The Styles of Interaction

There are at least four recognized styles of verbal interaction, including 'conversation', 'dialogue', 'apologetics' and 'confrontation'. Although not intrinsically 'Christian', all four are biblically permissible for Christians when used wisely and well. If we were to create another word picture to convey a national pattern, we could imagine that all the Christian/Muslim interaction in Britain is reduced to ten people. In that scenario, six of them are interacting via regular 'conversation' and social action, three have moved conversations on to use 'dialogue' and an 'apologetic' style, while only one is interacting in a 'confrontational' style.

Some might conclude from this illustration that the bigger the number of those engaged, the better, but it is not that simple. It is not a case of which is *best*, but of which is *appropriate* with whom and when. This is important because the 1 out of 10 who are confrontational in style are engaging like this online with radical individuals, and their interaction is being followed by hundreds of thousands of like-minded radicals around the world. This is more coverage than is achieved by the other nine combined.

That said, despite the small *quantity* of people who follow such arguments online, the discussion speaks to a narrower clientele at the assertive end of the spectrum, which requires a very specialized response from the Christians willing to enter that domain. Instead of criticizing this minority of Christians, there is a need to pray and urge them to abide by the same principles we will see for the other interactional styles. As the apostle Paul said: 'God has not given us a spirit of . . . *timidity* but of . . . *love* and *self-discipline*' (2 Tim. 1:7 NLT). When we set out the four styles as a list, we may spot the complementarity, as shown in Table 1.

Table 1 Four styles of verbal interaction

Style	Focus	Aim
Conversation	as people	build initial relationship and trust, open interaction
Dialogue	as people	identify and understand differences, be cooperative and two-way, listen to understand, question
Apologetics	as religions	clarify differences, explain, defend truth claims, be cooperative, deliver information
Confrontation	as religions	debate, refute criticisms, combat any inaccuracy, rebut false accusations, point out flaws in the other's truth claim

We should not think of these styles as four separate activities that can only be used one at a time. That is possible; however, human inter-action is usually fluid and tends to meander in and out of the styles as the conversation takes it. In any one interaction, several styles, or even all four, may emerge. It makes me think of the colours on an artist's palette which are mixed to create a unique picture. I remember a private discussion I had with a devout and assertive Muslim man with a white skullcap and beard. At the start of the conversation he was tense and on edge and wanting to get down to the business of cri-tiquing Christianity. It was clear that normal 'conversation' would not be possible because he was being 'confrontational'. I stepped up to the plate to address his criticisms by batting back to him the implied con-tradictions and misinformation that appeared to be driving his think-ing. My polite rebuttal seemed to earn his respect, which enabled us to move back through the gears to more amiable explanations (i.e.

apologetics). When the atmosphere became more relaxed we were able to compare notes (i.e. dialogue), before ending with general chit-chat (i.e. conversation). We used all four styles but in reverse order of intensity. This fluidity will always occur because we are all influenced by our lived experience, our personality, temperament, background, and any prior perceptions or assumptions about the other participant's position.

We now move on to evaluate the four styles, asking of each:

- What is it?
- Where does it come from?
- Why engage in it?
- How biblical is it?
- What are its strengths and weaknesses?
- What does 'good' and 'bad' use of it look like in practice?

1. Conversation as Christian Witness – Informal Introductions

'Conversation' is the most common style and is usually a one-to-one, informal and relational way of interacting. It is natural and spontaneous and happens in everyday situations. It is *irenic* (i.e. peaceable) in tone and can become a precursor to intentional dialogue. It does not require training or expertise, other than being a human being with the ability to ask how someone is doing.

In my experience, the vast majority of active Christians are interacting with people of other faiths in this way, which is why I have spent so much time preparing resources aimed at facilitating basic conversation among neighbours, friends or work colleagues. Such interaction is untrained and may not be about faith issues; it serves rather to build trust, relationship and mutual awareness of one another. Jesus is titled 'the Word' (John 1:1), and he consistently modelled 'conversation'. The Gospel of John is a catalogue of conversations, and among its most striking examples of Jesus' conversations are those he had with the majority immigrant community of his day – the Samaritans.

2. Dialogue in Christian Witness – Share, Define and Clarify Beliefs

Natural conversation can be a natural precursor to something more intentional, which we call 'dialogue'. This can happen either one-to-one over a cup of tea, or in a small group of those who are already sufficiently acquainted. The aim of dialogue is a *two-way* sharing, where one participant speaks while the other listens and responds. If used in a group, things work best on a slightly more organized footing, for instance, dialoguing about some clear and understood topic. Any group dynamic is helped by having a moderator to hold people to a time allocation and keep the topic on track.

Dialogue with people of other faiths

If it is a public dialogue with multicultural participants, it also helps to have questions written down and handed in beforehand, rather than leaving it open to observers (i.e. open mic), because dialogue may be understood by westerners but is not generally understood as a way of discourse in some cultures. For example, because the text of the Qur'an itself is couched in polemic assertions, it is more natural for many Muslims to assert things, which can come over to westerners as dogmatic. This is why some Muslims may *use* the word 'dialogue' but are actually referring to 'debate'. For people from Muslim backgrounds, dialogue can also be seen as a game of two halves; that is, they may invite a Christian to speak first, but then spend the rest of the time in a one-way rebuttal of Christian teaching, rather than giving an account of Islamic teaching.

Frank (Christian 'B' above) and his Muslim friends may be less keen on dialogue because they have their eye on the goal of persuading the other participant of their views, which reduces the interaction to a genteel kind of debate. Dialogue aims to achieve two things: first 'hearing', and second 'understanding'. It is the ground clearance to remove the rubble of misperception so that something new can be built. For Christians, dialogue is not just *about* our faith, saying that Jesus is good news (i.e. gospel); rather, to speak about him is to metaphorically lift Jesus up, which enables him to 'draw all people to [himself]' (John 12:32), also with the expectation that Scripture 'will not return . . . empty, but will . . . achieve the purpose for which [God] sent it' (Isa. 55:11). So, what does dialogue actually mean?

Defining dialogue

The word 'dialogue' comes from the Greek *dialegomai*, which is simply a verbal exchange between participants about an issue, which could be social, political or religious. The word is made up of two parts: *dia* meaning 'through' and *logos* meaning 'word'. Dialogue is therefore to interact through words in a two-way interaction. We say it is *irenic* because that term is based on the Greek word *eirēnē* (peace) which has been linked to the priest and scholar Erasmus (1466–1536), who brought together Christians who held different opinions and helped them to interact in ways that were peaceful, moderate and conciliatory. If the interaction slips into diatribe or debate, it stops being dialogue.

Without dialogue, the historic baggage between Christianity and Islam will clutter up the interaction and steer it in fruitless directions. This may be why Christian organizations such as the Lausanne Movement for World Evangelization (co-founded by Billy Graham) describe the urgent need for dialogue, particularly with regard to Christian interaction with Muslims:

> Not all Christian interaction with Muslims has been wise or loving. Some have misrepresented and belittled Muslims during the era of Western political and financial dominance . . . Many Christians were indifferent to the need to reduce mistrust and misunderstandings . . . appearing to be unconcerned about the deterioration of Christian values in the 'Christian world', and even openly supporting the secularization of the 'Muslim world'. This is evidence of 'cultural imperialism', coupled with aggressive and insensitive proselytism. Much within the modern mission movement needs rectifying.[2]

This is much-needed advice for all Protestants, but particularly for evangelicals, who may think of dialogue as theologically liberal – partly because Roman Catholics were doing it for centuries before it reached the agenda of Protestants, whose raison d'être is rooted in 'protest'. Because of this misunderstanding, I prefer to use the term 'proclamatory dialogue', which reflects the fact that dialogue is a sharing of one's belief, whether done individually or in a group.

An example of 'group dialogue' is Scriptural Reasoning, which did not emerge until as late as the 1990s when Jewish, Christian and Muslim academics began to join with leaders and interested 'lay' people from the three faiths of the 'Abrahamic' tradition. These groups meet in neutral venues and seek to safeguard 'integrity', 'honesty', 'respect', 'collegiality' and 'friendship'. The aim is to 'seek a better *quality* of disagreement' through the mutual reading aloud and questioning of one another's Scriptures, namely the Jewish Tanakh (the Christian Old Testament), the Christian New Testament and the Muslim Qur'an.[3]

How biblical is dialogue?

Dialogue is seen as an internal conversation with ourselves (Luke 12:17), as well as an externalized interaction with others (Matt. 16:7–8). It is also seen as a way of 'reasoning' (Acts 17:2,17; 18:4,19). Some of my favourite examples are Jesus' conversations throughout the Gospel of John, in which he dialogued with an enquiring Pharisee (John 3), a socially dysfunctional woman (John 4), a critical Jewish public (John 5; 7), his own fledgling followers (John 6), the Jewish hierarchy (John 8; 9; 10), some visiting Greeks (John 12) and his own inner circle of friends (John 13 – 17).

Dialogue is an open agenda

Christians such as Frank (Christian 'B' above) – not to mention the many Muslims who agree with him – would see dialogue as a 'soft option' for those who are 'conflict averse'. For them, dialogue is only useful when it enables them to set out their position without being interrupted. Such people are less comfortable with having to wait their turn in a two-way interaction where both participants are required to hear someone else out, including listening to what they consider to be erroneous.

On the other hand, Christians such as Lesley (Christian 'A' above) would want us to be careful to keep in mind Isaiah's words: 'a bruised reed [Messiah] will not break' (Isa. 42:3), and the apostle Paul's encouragement to 'speak' the truth in 'love' (Eph. 4:15). Such Christians see at least five reasons why dialogue should be taken seriously:

1. If we are certain of the truth of the gospel, we have nothing to fear from hearing other people explain their beliefs; it enables us to explain how Christian faith relates specifically to the other person.
2. It is a question of courtesy to the other participant.
3. It is being willing to walk alongside people to share their lives as part of a *process* of witness.
4. The other person wants to share what is precious to them too.
5. If we do not listen carefully to someone, we will misconstrue what they *actually* believe, and therefore fail to make our belief relevant and accessible to them. We might even find that their view may be unorthodox in their own tradition, or that it *is* orthodox yet similar to our own belief.

The possibility of either participant changing their position (i.e. *converting*) is a possibility, and good practice is to intentionally leave this open as a possible outcome. The scholar and author Bill Musk describes 'the search for the subliminal dynamics of the faith of a friend; it helps attune us to their mental wavelength so we can feel our way into their heart'.[4] This is crucial if Muslims and Christians are not to talk past each other, which often happens with words such as 'God', 'heaven', 'sin', 'salvation' or 'forgiveness'. These words may be used in both traditions, but they are used to mean markedly different things. It is important to note that Christianity and Islam agree on many peripheral aspects of faith such as creation, stewardship of the planet and a deistic outlook on life, while Islam rejects core tenets of the Christian faith such as the deity of Christ, the incarnation, the cross, redemption and the Trinity. When we can agree on the meaning of terms, it becomes easier to discuss the complex issues they refer to.

When dialogue is done well

When done well, dialogue:

- helps tease out the disparities between us as well as the 'miss-communication' they cause (according to Chawkat Moucarry, it is 'not only compatible with biblical Christian witness; it is inseparable'[5])
- is not the sole prerogative of those at the 'liberal' end of the theological spectrum
- is a prelude *to* a gospel conversation, not a substitute *for* it
- keeps the door open for further conversations
- helps us know one another better and appreciate one another as human beings
- avoids joining strident Muslims in the slanging match some of them crave
- allows both participants to receive as much via their *heart* as via their head
- can be learned on the job, as it only requires us to speak of what we know
- can be adopted by a Muslim because of the Qur'anic instruction: 'Do not argue with People of the Book but *in the best possible way*, except in the case of those among them who have been unjust' (see Qur'an 29:46; cf. 3:64; 16:125), in which the expression 'best possible way' (*bi-llati hiya ahsan*) means 'having a good relationship', 'dealing courteously and gently', recognizing that God revealed the Bible to Jews and Christians first; the 'best possible way' creates the possibility that 'your enemy will become like a close friend' (Qur'an 41:34).[6]

When dialogue is done badly

When done badly, dialogue:

- backfires due to the approach of some Muslims who choose to view all Christians as unworthy of the 'best possible way' because they see them all as 'those . . . who have been unjust' (Qur'an 29:46)
- can give the impression that it is only suitable for the more experienced or scholarly, but this is not true – it is for *all* and should be done at the appropriate level both parties want to bring to it (for example, one Christian woman told me: 'I had never heard of the world "dialogue" – I just started chatting with Muslim women')
- loses its integrity and becomes a form of entrapment, or is a ruse to an undisclosed end (to avoid this, both participants need to ask questions that are honest and open, with no hidden agenda)
- can drift away from 'proclamatory dialogue' to protect the relationship with the other participant – people may be tempted to only compare common ground and become woolly on points of disagreement
- turns into a need to 'save face', making it less *natural* (this may happen if more than one Muslim is present)
- can be mistaken for, or even become, 'ecumenical' or 'interfaith' (i.e. theologically liberal)
- may not be respected by confrontational Muslims, who need something more robust.

The bottom line is that any interaction which ignores dialogue can appear patronizing, while dialogue without a clear articulation of belief can become an academic or superficial exercise; but 'proclamatory dialogue' makes interaction more informative, meaningful and effective. Dialogue therefore is the necessary spadework to 'prepare the way for the LORD' (Isa. 40:3).

If 'conversation' acts as a precursor to 'dialogue', we find that dialogue is also a natural precursor to 'apologetics'.

3. Apologetics in Christian Witness – Explain and Defend

Good dialogue can lead naturally in and out of the 'apologetic' style, which is also versatile because it works well one-to-one, or in a small group or in a larger public gathering. Like dialogue, the format is tailored to suit the context, and the bigger the group, the more need for a moderator to keep things on track. Like dialogue, it is an irenic form of interaction; however, it also has the capacity to be more *robust* if the other participant needs that. This enables apologetics to sit in the middle ground between the 'dialogue' and 'confrontational' styles.

What is apologetics?

The word 'apologetics' comes from the Greek word *apologia*, which is made up of two parts: *apo* (from) and *logos* (conversation). Its aim is simply to give a *reasoned* reply to questions from others. It also carries the sense of verbally defending something. This sort of defence is not military and physical; it is a *legal* defence (i.e. a reasoned explanation).

To interact 'apologetically' requires a search for new ways of phrasing things to help the other participant understand what we mean; this is why Jesus used parables. Questions are best left open-ended, for instance: 'Why does this matter to you?'[7] This way, we get a response that will tell us as much about the person as it does about their disagreement with our position. Another example of an open question is: 'Where in the Qur'an/Bible does it say [such and such]?' This helps to keep the conversation earthed in the *source* of an argument, as opposed to putting forward hearsay, bias or inaccuracy in an argument.

Apologetics can be done through lectures, written articles or blogs, and increasingly through online presentations. Some prominent Christians who have championed apologetics with Muslims include Martin Accad (Lebanon), Michael Ramsden (Ravi Zacharias Ministries), Andy Bannister (Solas) and Michael Brown and Josh McDowell (USA).

How biblical is apologetics?

Apologetics is a rich theme in the New Testament pattern of witness.

Jesus

Jesus used this style in response to the frequent questions put to him by his hearers; some were genuine enquirers and others antagonistic. We have already mentioned his interactions with Nicodemus (John 3) and the Samaritan woman (John 4). It could also be argued that Jesus' teaching in the Sermon on the Mount (Matt. 5 – 7) is an apologetic response to the Pharisees' legalistic interpretation of the Sabbath. He raises the bar on the truth contained in law-based religion to the spiritual dynamic of grace. He also corrects them by saying: 'The Sabbath was made for man, not man for the Sabbath' (Mark 2:23–28; cf. 27). It happens again when he challenges the Sadducees' interpretation of the resurrection of the dead. He concludes: 'Are you not in error because you do not know the Scriptures or the power of God?' (Mark 12:18–27; cf. 24).

Jesus is masterful when he argues about whose son the Christ is, concluding: 'If then David calls [Christ] "Lord", how can [Christ] be [King David's] son?' (Matt. 22:42–44; cf. 45). He combined reason with the thrust or text of the Scripture, using arguments that ought to resonate with the hearer.

Philip

There seems to be enough consistency among the words and lifestyle of the apostles of Christ to assume that apologetics was part of their practice, if not a tenet of the 'apostles' teaching' (Acts 2:42). This may well have been the case, judging by the actions of Philip, the deacon from the church in Jerusalem, who gave an apologetic explanation to an Ethiopian civil servant of what the Scriptures say about the sufferings of Messiah (Acts 8:26–40).

The apostle Peter

Peter's explanation to his fellow Jews in his Pentecost sermon is an example of apologetic (Acts 2:14–41). In his letters he gives guidance on what followers of Christ could do when they are falsely accused and questioned by hostile people. The non-negotiable requirement for Peter may be: 'in your hearts honour Christ the Lord as holy, always being prepared to make a defence to anyone who asks you for a reason for the hope that is in you; yet do it with gentleness and respect' (1 Pet. 3:15 ESV).

The apostle Paul

Paul gave an apologetic argument to his fellow Jews at the synagogue in Damascus after his conversion (Acts 9:2–22), and again when he used his personal testimony in Jerusalem to a majority-Jewish crowd (Acts 22), and then again at a meeting of the Sanhedrin Council (Acts 23). He also used apologetics when he conveyed the gospel to *non-Jews* in a Gentile gathering at the home of Cornelius, an Italian military officer (Acts 10). Paul modelled the use of apologetics in three distinct ways, as follows:

1. He *reasoned* the case for Christ among Jews and Greeks (Acts 13:16–43; 18:4–5; 28:23–31), which is closer to the dialogue end of this spectrum.
2. He also gave a legal *defence* (i.e. explanation) of the claims of Christ (Phil. 1:7,16), which is in the apologetics area of the spectrum. He did this again before Festus, when Paul's legal rights as a Roman citizen were being called into question (Acts 25). He did it yet again to *defend* himself when his credentials as an apostle were being challenged (1 Cor. 9:1–3).
3. He used *robust persuasion* to influence people for Christ (2 Cor. 5:11), sometimes in ways that were closer to the 'confrontational' end of the spectrum.

I remember apologetics being effective when I was invited to take an assembly in one of the largest Deobandi Islamic boys' schools in Britain. It felt like an Islamic Hogwarts because over 200 teenagers, clad in white prayer caps and gowns, sat cross-legged on the carpeted mosque floor (the school hall). They listened with rapt attention as I explained the significance of the season of Lent and the Easter story, based on Abraham's call to sacrifice his son (Gen. 22:1–19). The students knew the story from the Qur'an, which has a sketchy account of the ram caught in the thicket. Mount Moriah, the site of this incident, is none other than the area in which the crucifixion of Jesus took place. As the Lamb of God (John 1:29), he became the embodiment of the ram that enabled Abraham's son to be spared.

When apologetics is done well

Good practice in apologetics:

- flows naturally in and out of dialogue, keeping the door of conversation open, paving the way for sharing
- seeks mental connection (i.e. engaging the head), which in turn helps foster trust (i.e. engaging the heart)
- helps compare and contrast the positions of both participants
- allows difficult things to be said tactfully: 'The one who has knowledge uses words with restraint, and whoever has understanding is even-tempered' (Prov. 17:27)
- requires a right attitude in the individuals using it.

When apologetics is done badly

When done badly, apologetics:

- can become sterile due to the rehearsing of tired arguments on topics that are not of mutual interest

- can slip into personal passion, which can become heated and tip over into acrimony (especially in public debate)
- is more likely than dialogue to touch soft spots in either participant, which may provoke a combative response
- may involve correcting a Muslim in a clumsy way, thus violating their sense of 'honour' and being perceived as imposing 'shame' on them, which is tantamount to the demolition of their essential *being* and can embitter them towards the person thought to have inflicted the shame (this can happen because, while a westerner may accept a correction and learn from it, someone with an 'eastern' mindset may not, particularly when an audience is present)
- can be discouraging, particularly in the hands of beginners who may get out of their depth.

Many active Muslims and Christians become passionate when interacting on issues they care deeply about, which is not a *bad* thing. However, there are several other possible reasons why passion is often expressed by Muslims. It could be:

- an aspect of their culture and/or temperament, which may look like *aggression* to a western eye
- an expression of frustration, or even personal hurt, resulting from issues we have covered in earlier chapters
- a reaction to a perceived slight on their 'honour', causing them to feel they have 'lost face'
- a reaction to a paradigm shift going on inside them due to the new incoming information, which was the case when the radical Pharisee Saul of Tarsus hit out at followers of Jesus and was told: 'it is hard for you to kick against the goads' (Acts 26:14)
- a mixture of any of the above.

The point here is not to assume that passion or agitation is aggression.

Lesley (Christian 'A' above) might feel intimidated by an emotional reaction in her gentle line of work, while Frank (Christian 'B' above) would most likely see the passion as evidence of a real connection with the other participant. It seems to me that the comfort or discomfort triggered by assertive people probably contributes to a wariness about confrontation, but we need to face the reality that in some cultures (my own family included) it is the preferred style. Passionate individuals may prefer to bypass the 'Nicodemus' motif of conversation, dialogue and apologetics, in favour of the 'David and Goliath' motif of robust apologetics or confrontation.

It seems realistic to recognize that irenic styles of interaction have their limitations in the current climate. Christian faith-interaction that is irenic is never likely to impact a certain type of Muslim who has a more assertive (even aggressive) outlook and a need to interact in the more adversarial way that is familiar to them.

Stephen

I have saved till last the apologetic discourse of Stephen, the first Christian martyr. He followed Jesus' example when responding to legalistic religionists after his arrest, in that his defence speech starts off as an apologetic outline of Israelite history and how the Mosaic tradition came into being. However, when he gets to the death of Christ as Messiah, he changes gear to what might be described as 'robust apologetics' (Acts 7:47 – 8:3). I mention this now because *robust* apologetics (whoever it is used with) is a more combative expression of apologetics and is a natural precursor to the 'confrontational' style, which we will now look at.

4. Confrontation in Christian Witness – Defend and Press an Argument Home

I am puzzled to find that when atheists and anti-Christian propagators such as Richard Dawkins or the late Christopher Hitchens attack the Bible and the validity of Christianity, we applaud active Christians such as Professor John Lennox for stepping forward to debate them on issues such as the existence of God and the scientific flaws in the Darwinian world view. However, when a Christian steps forward to debate a Muslim propagator who strays beyond the limits of Muslim decency to attack the Bible and Christianity, that Christian is criticized and accused of being 'less than Christian' – I have done so myself.

The confrontational style has a 'Marmite' reputation – people seem to either love it or hate it, affirm it or avoid it. We must be open to the words of Paul who said: 'Let God transform you into a new person by changing the way you think. Then you will learn to know God's will for you, which is good and pleasing and perfect' (Rom. 12:2 NLT). We have already seen that vexing issues, such as 'political correctness', cannot be assessed in a binary way as either good or bad; some issues can be either, depending on how they are used. When we grasp this, we have the mental and verbal tools with which to assess confrontational interaction, and then we must think through the following four questions:

- Is 'confrontational' interaction *necessary* in the current climate?
- Is it a *valid* style?
- Is it *appropriate* for use by active Christians?
- Can the style be used with *integrity*, that is, within the biblical parameters of 'grace and truth'?

Is confrontational interaction necessary in the current climate?

The mountains we have been describing have deposited their toxic residue into our psyche and polluted it to the point where some recognized social commentators wonder where the line of no return is in society, and fear that we may have crossed it already. The toxic waste of Mount Strident can be seen in populism, ultra-nationalism, the weaponization of political correctness, dangerous religion run amuck, more interrogative forms of interview in mainstream media (i.e. press, TV and radio), adversarial politics and strident behaviour in social media. Western societies are now an exercise in hyper-democracy where everyone has a say about everything and we are making up the rules as we go along; it is therefore a noisier household where you have to speak up to be heard and the only way to get a word in edgeways is to speak compellingly, with clarity and wisdom. Christians have both at their disposal but persist in speaking among themselves.

If we are to navigate Mount Correct (i.e. the sinister use of political correctness), Mount Strident (i.e. intolerant and binary thinking) and Mount Occlusion (i.e. the ideology behind dangerous religion), it is necessary in our day to ensure that the repertoire of interactive styles includes confrontation.

Is confrontation a valid style?

Even if confrontation is *necessary*, it does not always make it *valid*. There are still reservations, particularly among some northern Europeans, particularly many Christians. It is my contention that this reaction is more cultural than biblical. I say this because the Bible (like the Qur'an) is a culturally Semitic document, reflecting the cultural distinctives of the Middle East, which is why, on occasion, Jesus engaged with people confrontationally. The point here is that the principles of cross-cultural interaction include not just couching your truth in terms that are accessible to the other participant, but also presenting it in a style that is normative for them. Westerners are more comfortable with the first than the second, which I believe is primarily a *cultural* discomfort. The Jewish debater Rabbi Isser Z. Weisberg confirms that adversarial interaction is normative among Jews (as it is among Arabs). He cites the disagreements among the scholars in the Talmud, arguing that individual Jews are adversarial and argumentative, and that Bible characters such as Moses and Job even behaved this way with God.[8]

Weisberg has debated on various subjects, including the atheistic beliefs of fellow Jews such as Sam Harris; the historic treatment of Jews by Christians; social issues such as sexual minorities; violence in the pursuit of the Black Lives Matter ideology; the Christian/Muslim claim that Jesus existed and that he is the Messiah; and the beliefs of Islamist Muslims. Other prominent names are debating *for* and *against* issues, both internally within a group and externally between different groups; the trending issues include things such as climate change, human rights, modernity, the veracity of the opinions of some scholars, and the search for democratic principles in the Global South.

Is confrontation appropriate for active Christians?

I am pressing this point here because, whether we agree or disagree with confrontational interaction, active Christians who have not been persuaded of this tend to be conspicuous by their absence in public discourse with Muslims, be that public debate, written material or online video footage. Training for Christian 'ministry' revolves around the Christendom model of 'church gathered' in a building – the 'boat *in* which to fish' during the holy hour of the faithful. However, society has changed, so to be effective in its social function as 'moral salt and spiritual light' (see Matt. 5:13–16) the urgent call to 'the church' is for new approaches that will facilitate 'church scattered' in society from Monday to Friday. In this model, the church is a 'boat *from* which to fish'.

Christian values will remain conspicuous by their absence in public discourse until Christian denominations consider public discourse as a new strategic mission frontier, which needs not only ministers and youth workers but also trained and salaried full-time social analysts, commentators and communicators. These are the people who are crucial at the borders of current affairs and biblical theology. The lack of such people means that Christian values have little voice, and journalists and news channels struggle to find reliable Christians who are able and willing to comment or challenge current views in ways that sidestep the landmines of PC rules, to contribute positively to the national conversation. As it is, the 'church gathered' paradigm causes the 'church' to be like a benign pastor of a recalcitrant and self-absorbed society where people are *not* primarily asking whether Christianity is 'true' (in some absolute sense) but what difference it would make to their lives if they embraced it.

Confronting entrenched ideas becomes both *necessary* in the current climate and *valid* if the high priests of political correctness are to be challenged in their agenda to erode the Judeo-Christian heritage. It is ironic that it is not active Christians who are engaging these people; rather, the challenge is coming from articulate individuals whose lives are influenced by the Judeo-Christian heritage but who are agnostic or atheist, such as Jordan Peterson, Douglas Murray and Stephen Fry. They may even be Jewish, such as Sam Harris and Ben Shapiro.

Can a confrontational style be used with integrity?

If confrontation in public discourse is a fact of life in eastern society, it has become more prevalent in western society too. Whether we like it or not, the 'gloves are coming off' in the West and issues that were historically taboo to talk about (let alone challenge) are now being scrutinized openly. It is in this context that confrontational interaction has come to the fore.

This has been happening across the Arabic-speaking world over the past three decades, as Mount Occlusion led to the so-called 'Arab Spring', the destabilization of fascist groups such as ISIS, and the migrant flow of refugees – all of which were spurred on by the internet. It is therefore in the Middle East that online confrontational interaction has had one of its most significant impacts. An example among Christians is the Egyptian Coptic priest Abouna Zakaria, who took on the majority view in 2008 by setting up the Al Hayat satellite TV channel, which is now reaching 60 million viewers. He has also set up internet chat rooms staffed by teams of people who engage with audience reactions, questions and enquiries. Born in Alexandria, Abouna Zakaria was active when I lived in Egypt in the 1980s; at that time he would speak with the eloquence of Apollos of Alexandria (Acts 18:24), the irresistible wisdom of Stephen (Acts 6:10) and the same erudition in Islamics that Paul had in Judaism. It is estimated that tens of thousands of Egyptians have changed their allegiance from Islam to Jesus Christ as a result of Zakaria's forthright and blunt argument, which is why he was jailed for life (though later released into permanent exile).[9] Due to the internet, Zakaria has had more impact while living *outside* the Arab world than he did when he lived *in* it.

While we may be in awe of such people, we must remember that debating face-to-face, in writing or online is a *specialist* calling. To help the active Christians who perceive confrontation to be antithetical to 'the way of Christ', I prefer to refer to the confrontational style as '*robust* apologetics'. This is a concession to those whose problem may well prove to be one of western cultural sensibility, which sees Jesus as the quintessential gentleman rather than the Middle Easterner he was. He could be *very* confrontational at times; agreed, this was with his fellow Jews who were part of a culpable professional religious elite leading others astray. We will see in a moment that the same was also evident in the apostle Paul's interaction when challenging people both inside and outside the Christian community.

I used to have a blind spot in that I was subconsciously trying to offer Jesus and Paul a cloak of respectability to cover the fact that they exhibited 'un-British' behaviour by challenging others. To say Jesus *only* confronted his fellow Jews is to admit he *was* confrontational when necessary; so the question is not *whether* confrontation is appropriate, but *when*, *why* and *how*. It seems to me that the confrontational style is indeed appropriate, so long as we define clearly what we mean by it and the scope of its use.

While confrontational debate is frowned on by some and applauded by others, it is important to unpack the quandary and redress the imbalance, so I have given it enough word space to enable a fair hearing alongside the other styles.

What is 'confrontational' interaction?

In a word, we are saying that 'robust apologetics' or 'confrontational' interaction are both referring to *debate*. Debate emerged in the ancient world and was championed by people such as Socrates and Plato and has become part of the democratic process we recognize today. If the apologetic style *explains* and *defends* a position, the confrontational style utilizes facts, not just about our own argument but also about the flaws in the other participant's argument. It seeks to *robustly* defend a position against robust intellectual attack. It seeks to *refute* inaccuracies, untruths or misinformation about our argument, and to *expose* the flaws in the other argument; and even (where necessary) to go on the offensive (without *being* offensive!) to press home the counter-argument.

How helpful is the word 'polemics'?

The confrontational style is also a 'Cinderella' among the styles because of the use (mostly in North America) of the word 'polemics' to refer to 'confrontation' as understood in the continent of Europe, including the UK. This has made the issue a proverbial elephant in the room, particularly for evangelical Christians. We will unpack this difference in a moment. It helps me to think of the word 'polemics' as offering and defending an argument that is the *polar* opposite of the other participant.

The original root meaning (etymology) of the word 'polemic' is the Greek word *polemos* (war), which is the opposite of *eirēnē* (peace), which is the dominant characteristic of the other styles, namely conversation, dialogue and apologetics. 'Polemic' can be defined as a strongly worded written or verbal attack on someone or something. This is less than positive, which is why some Christians understandably argue that the word is 'un-Christian'. However, other Christians see three things:

1. The word 'polemic' is used metaphorically about arguments, *not* literally as war on people.
2. 'Polemic' is a traditional adjective used to describe debate that is adversarial, combative or confrontational.

3. Applied linguistics shows that a sign of a *living* language is that the meaning of a word can develop a popular meaning which diverges from the original dictionary definition. For example, the word 'pretty' morphed from the original negative connotation of 'crafty' or 'cunning', to mean 'clever' or 'elegant', 'delicate' and even 'diminutive'. The word 'awful' has morphed from its original connotation of 'fear', 'terror' and 'dread', to connote something that is 'awesome'; this is a shift away from something worthy of 'reverential fear', to its current sense of 'impressive'. When such shifts in meaning happen, dictionaries adapt by tracing the historic root of a word as well as the contemporary sense in which it is being used.

This helps us with the fact that the *meaning* being brought to the word 'polemic' today (by those who use it) has changed, at least in its North American usage where the word is interchangeable with 'robust apologetics'. The difference in meaning on either side of the Atlantic Ocean is therefore quite distinct. The reasons for this seem rooted in the respective history and culture of America and Britain, which shape our respective world views.

The sense attached to 'polemic' in the UK today

The British psyche is more naturally aligned with *persuasion*. This characterizes its national discourse, including its parliamentary process, which is orientated towards the 'conversion' of the other's position. People are persuaded to change their view by a better argument. As a result, the majority of British Christians (including evangelicals) could be described as having the gentle and winsome persuasiveness of Lesley (Christian 'A' above).

British Christians tend to be culturally *irenic* in outlook, which plays out in the way they perceive what is *normative* in interaction with Muslims. Perhaps most British Christians struggle to use the word 'polemic', while a significant minority of 'ultra-conservative' evangelicals embrace a more conflict-based paradigm, albeit expressed in a more reserved way than in the USA. The whole of Europe is aware that we are in a post-colonial era, which means that when British Christians understand the etymology of the word 'polemics', there is an inevitable instinct to shy away from using the word, let alone seeing it as a valid approach to the Great Commission of Christ.

The sense attached to 'polemic' in the USA today

The UK and the USA are divided by more than a common language, they are two distinct cultures. The American national psyche appears to be more *adversarial* than the British, to say the least. Take, for instance, how political discourse is done in the USA and how, for many, evangelicalism has become almost like another political party. This cultural pattern can cause gasps in Britons, who are faced with the reality that this sort of interaction seems to be a normal part of the American psyche; this also helps to explain the culture of litigation and support for the right to bear arms and an approval of military intervention. It may also explain why most conservative American evangelicals would be more aligned with the views of Frank (Christian 'B' above) than with Lesley (Christian 'A' above). When we look at the websites of American conservative Evangelical and Reformed organizations, we find they are likely to be more right-wing, truth-dominant and conflict-oriented in outlook than is generally the case in the UK and mainland Europe.

What many American conservative evangelicals share with their British counterparts is a strong orientation towards 'verbal proclamation', which is where a confrontational style sits. An adversarial orientation also means a lower regard for decorum, something that is more widely valued in the UK. In fact, my American friends tell me that the psyche of most American evangelicals is influenced by a paradigm of war or conflict, which is supported by the way they understand the Bible.

Many prominent evangelical pundits in America are not only polemic in *tone* but even 'anti-irenic', seeing conciliation as weak. Over the last generation, these voices have won over the majority of American evangelicals to that sort of outlook, which has been undergirded by the Trump years. Therefore, the concept of 'polemics' resonates more easily with the cultural and social sensibilities of Americans. My recommended read on this issue would be the book *The Certainty Trap* by Bishop Bill Musk,[10] which looks at the striking similarity between Muslim and Christian 'conservatives' in that they start from a very different place regarding the inspiration of their respective Scriptures but arrive at the same place, namely that their Scriptures can only be understood properly through a *literalist* lens, and that revelation is essentially 'fixed' and 'closed' rather than a developmental and 'living' conversation with the divine. This also seems to be at the heart of the discomfort with modernity felt in both traditions. Such transatlantic differences are the reason the UK tends to reflect the outlook of Lesley (Christian 'A' above); and why they feel drawn to the 'Good Samaritan' motif of *care* as a sign of Christ, while the USA tends to reflect the outlook of Frank (Christian 'B' above) and may feel drawn to a 'John the Baptist' motif – of *challenge* as a sign of Christ. Again, I suggest this difference is rooted as much in cultural *preference* as it is in theological conviction. This is why I prefer the word 'confrontational', because it provides a platform on which we can *all* meet to at least think about the issues.

While some passionate Muslims and Christians are proud to call themselves 'polemicists', and while most Americans accept the word 'polemics', and members of the academic community use it, I accept the word as a fact of life but with the proviso that we rehabilitate the meaning by identifying what 'good' and 'bad' practice looks like in confrontational interaction.

What bad confrontation looks like

Elsewhere in the book, I have mentioned some poor behaviour among zealous evangelicals, but my worst example of bad practice was when I attended a Christian debate involving the world-renowned Muslim debater, the late Ahmed Deedat, who was vitriolic in attitude, bombastic in tone, and blasphemous in his insinuations about Jesus (even in Islamic terms). He attacked Christ, Christianity and the character of the Christian debater. While this was going on, I shared my New Testament with a Kuwaiti guy sitting next to me. We would check the references being used. We sat shaking our heads in disbelief at Deedat's behaviour and that of the bellowing audience, which included some Christians.

At another debate, Professor Lee Chai Peng, a Malaysian Christian, asked Deedat why he attacked Christianity as unliveable in practice. In response Deedat called him to the platform and slapped his face, saying: 'Now turn the other cheek. That's your faith.' The largely Muslim audience was restless and so Deedat said: 'OK, let's prove this point quickly'. He asked Professor Lee to remove his shirt, and then demanded: 'Aren't you supposed to give me your trousers too?' The professor apologized to his students in the audience and declared: 'My faith in Christ is real and I want to show this man how real it is to me.' He then took off the items of clothing and went back to his office, where he found a queue of his Muslim students waiting to apologize for Deedat's behaviour.[11] Deedat's attitude, words and actions were beyond confrontational and unacceptable.

I have also viewed 'bad' debaters online who come over as blink-ered, closed to reason, rude, and taking cheap shots at Christianity based on twisted facts and warped logic. These include speakers such as Zakir Naik, Mohammed Hijab (who has a massive following of 390,000 YouTube subscribers) and Ali Dawah (who has 531,000 YouTube subscribers, which again is huge), individuals featured on the channels SCDawah (266,000 YouTube subscribers) and DawahMedia (81,500 subscribers), and the author Adnan Rashid (51,000 subscribers). I have found few 'good' Muslim debaters, but they are there in the form of people such as Sheikh Dr Shabir Ally.

Some common-sense guidelines to enhance the effectiveness of confrontational debate include the following:

1. It is only advisable for those who are properly trained.
2. It is an approach limited to the minority of radical Muslims.

3. It is limited culturally, for instance to the South Asian mindset.
4. It is not necessarily effective with *all* cultures.[12]
5. It is not for all Christians; for example, the British missionary Temple Gairdner of Cairo started out using it but found it hindered his situation and later said: 'We need the melodious note of song in our message to the Muslim . . . not the dry cracked note of disputation, but the song of joyous witness, and tender invitation'.[13]
6. It can overlook the fact that *all* forms of Christian witness have social implications, and all forms of social engagement by Christians *should* have spiritual implications (Rom. 12:17 – 13:10).
7. It can de-emphasize Jesus' mandate to make not just converts but '*disciples* [among] all nations' (Matt. 28:19).
8. It can send both participants away thinking they have 'won'.

What good confrontation looks like

Having put the above incidents to people who consider themselves to be 'polemicists', I have found that they too are horrified by such bad practice. One practitioner said: 'The confrontation is about holding the opposing argument to account, not abusing that participant in any way.' This is good advice we should *all* be more open to, especially in light of the subtle effects of western imperialism, hegemony and racism which can creep into Christian/Muslim interaction on both sides.

Good practice is modelled well by the mixed-race South African TV anchor and presenter Trevor Noah, who has mastered the art of *confronting* without being confrontational (in the bad sense); that is, he knows how to go on the offence without being 'offensive'. The aim is *not* to 'destroy' the other but to engage and invite them to change their mind. Noah is a joy to watch, so I looked into his approach and found it is modelled on what is known as the 'Socratic method', which is essentially an irenic form of debate where we seek to understand the other's argument and then frame our disagreement with the following in mind:

1. Find the hidden premise, namely, the concealed assumptions in the mind of the other participant.
2. Ask genuine questions rather than making statements. (Try to fully understand the other's position; do not see him or her as typical of many. Do not say 'So you are saying [such and such]', which can be putting words into their mouth; instead, ask probing questions, identifying inconsistencies in a non-accusatory way.)
3. Confidently defend your position without appearing antagonistic. (Say 'Yes, but . . .', which accepts common ground while pressing the opposing point; blunt rebuttal comes over as a put-down and can insult the opponent.)

When the above happens, it produces the following benefits:

1. It brings both participants onto a level playing field where they can only admit into evidence material that is sourced from their respective texts (i.e. the Bible or the Qur'an, Hadith, *sira*, *tafsir* and *tarikh*).
2. It earns the respect of a radical Muslim.
3. It corresponds with the views of John of Damascus (AD 655) who saw Islam as a sort of Judeo-Christian heresy[14] that is 'near' to the faith of Abraham, not 'far off' (Acts 2:39).
4. It can encourage the other participant to critique the historic, textual and ethical difficulties in their own tradition.

The rationale behind debate

The small band of Christian practitioners who debate tell me that part of their motivation is to challenge *bad* debaters; this is especially so with some Muslim debaters who can be aggressive and vitriolic.

This alone is not a reason, but it is important to realize that these people are influencing potentially millions of Muslims who follow them on social media platforms such as YouTube. It seems highly appropriate, if not crucial, that qualified Christians should step up to challenge such rhetoric and expose the flaws in the arguments that are used to attack Christianity. If Christians will not step up for this, who else will, or can? The issue is not whether Christians *should* get involved in this area, but *how* they should do so. Common sense suggests this should be done in a way that is worthy of Jesus Christ. When Christians engage with confrontational people (that is, on their turf), they should *not* do so in the same antagonistic spirit but instead set an example.

Experienced Christian practitioners of confrontational interaction argue that there is a real need to counter the ideology that undergirds Islamist violence because this is what is shutting down the minds of the younger generations to reason (including the possibility of considering the good news of Jesus Christ). It seems the greatest assistance that Christians could offer to the Muslim communities in the West would be to support the engagement of Christian specialists by joining fair-minded Muslims to confront the radical ideology that provokes strident reactions from the public. This would prevent people from assuming that all Muslims embrace a form of Islam that has not been reformed since the seventh century, and which is becoming increasingly anachronistic, totalitarian, misogynistic, blinkered and incompatible with modernity. Christian debaters are monitoring the following developments:[15]

1. the watershed created by the atttacks of 11 September 2001 (9/11) in the USA and 7 July 2005 (7/7) in the UK
2. the subsequent and ongoing Islamist attacks in the western world
3. the radicalization of younger Muslims that is feeding the terrorist attacks in the West
4. the proliferation of radical theology, with few Islamic scholars willing to challenge it openly

5. the inappropriateness of Christian mission agencies confronting the radical ideology
6. the climate of political correctness which avoids the issues and restricts any challenge.

Such Christian practitioners are aware that this is an essentially *political* analysis, but they see their calling as being in the tradition of people such as Aleksandr Solzhenitsyn and Dietrich Bonhoeffer, who confronted dominant ideologies in their day. They are going about their role by confronting the 'received' foundations of history, including where Mecca really was; whether Muhammad was a real person (or an amalgam of several people as in the Robin Hood figure); the claim that the Qur'an was perfectly preserved and why there are multiple versions today; the arguably pagan elements in Islam's roots, such as the veneration of Muhammad as being next only to God; and the pagan roots of the Kaaba.

One man's journey into polemic debating

I am indebted to Jay Smith, who is a prominent practitioner of confrontational Christian witness. Smith was born into an American Mennonite family. His parents were missionaries, so he was raised in northern India. He came to the UK from America in the 1990s and spent twenty-five years engaging with radical Muslims who were coming into the UK with the aim of discrediting Christianity and preparing the way for Islam in national life. The film footage of his open-air debates would be used to influence the rest of the Islamic world. It was in this context that Smith honed his craft at Speaker's Corner, Hyde Park in London, and in several university towns.

Muslims and Christians still debate face to face, but as the internet developed a shift took place towards online debates using social media platforms. This has brought them to a global audience of atheists, political groups, Muslims and Christians, among others.

An important impact of this shift is that 'everyday' Muslims in the heartlands of Islam are being exposed to the message of assertive Muslim polemicists, some of whom seem to focus entirely on attacking Christianity. This is emboldening everyday Muslims to adopt the same attitude and to challenge Christians with the same material they have seen online. Christians are unable to respond to the questions and they are seeking help – of which there is little available because the confrontational approach has so far been a Cinderella among the approaches to Christian witness.

The internet is the modern equivalent of the ancient places of commerce and debate, such as the Roman Forum or the Agora in Athens (the marketplace where Socrates debated ideas with people), the Areopagus (Acts 17:16–34) or the Hall of Tyrannus in Ephesus (Acts 19:9). Christian debaters, such as Jay Smith, have followed the action by creating an online presence to debate Muslims and to train Christians (particularly those under pressure in the Global South) who are asking to be taught 'apologetics and polemics'. Smith points out that western mission workers are unable to meet this need because it is not on their radar; they tend instead to persist with the irenic and relational approaches that are better suited to Muslim minorities in Europe and North America, but which are less appropriate in Muslim-majority countries or among Christian minorities faced with a growing Islamic influence.

How biblical is confrontation about truth?

Now it is time to test the material above against biblical examples of confrontational interaction in pursuit of conveying Christian truth. As with all the styles, we must resist the temptation to read *into* the Bible what we expect to see there (a process known as 'eisegesis'). The aim is to derive *from* the Bible what the text is *actually* saying (i.e. 'exegesis'). There are three guiding questions to bear in mind as we look at the texts below: first, *who* was being confronted; second, *what* were they confronted about; and third, *why*.

Jesus

In the Gospel of Matthew chapter 23, Jesus confronts some Pharisees. I see this incident as a reflection of how he might interact with a zealot of PC, a proponent of the new atheism, or a radical Muslim, each of whom might have a similar attitude and mindset to the Pharisees. Jesus accused these Jewish religionists of:

- turning God's life-giving law into a soul-destroying legalistic mind-game (vv. 16–24)
- setting a hypocritical example to the uninitiated (vv. 25–26)
- showing farcical zeal and exerting an erroneous influence on the masses by their doctrine (v. 15).

In the style of the Old Testament prophets, Jesus called the religious elite 'whitewashed tombs', meaning they had a nice exterior but were ugly inside (vv. 27–28), and 'snakes' who are 'condemned to hell' (see v. 33). He pronounced judgement on their ideology using hyperbole to threaten them with the prediction that all the innocent blood shed on earth would come on them (vv. 34–39).

It is interesting to note that there is no record of Jesus being confrontational with everyday immigrants, such as the Samaritans, even though they held to an aberrant form of Judaism – which provides a parallel with Islam which is a latecomer in the Judeo-Christian line. What I wish the Gospels included was evidence of Jesus interacting with Samaritan religious leaders, who were the curators of their hybrid form of Judaism that had pagan elements mixed in. To the extent that Islam is one of the 'faiths of Abraham', Christians and Muslims are 'spiritual cousins', which brings radical Muslim leaders into the scope of the sort of confrontational approach Jesus took with Pharisees in his day, because they had souls in their care.

Stephen

In chronological order, after Jesus is Stephen, the first Christian martyr, who was 'highly spoken of' (Acts 6:8–15). In Acts 7, Stephen

emulates his master, Rabbi Jesus, when he addresses the same religious
elite who had tried Jesus and were now putting *him* on trial. Stephen
even adopts some of the same behaviours as Jesus. He starts with an
'apologetic' overview of Israelite history (vv. 1–44) and ends with a
'confrontational' denunciation of the Judaic religious system that was
dominated by a religious elite who had rejected Jesus as Messiah (vv.
48–53). It is interesting that Islamic teaching accepts Jesus as Messiah
but rejects his *deity*. We cannot vouch for Stephen's *tone* because we
were not there, but what we do know is that it was direct in confronting the ideology that the religious professionals had created around
the law of Moses (Acts 7:9,27,35,39–43,51–53). What we do know is
that Stephen's words provoked fury in the audience, sealing his death
(Acts 6:9–10; 7:57 – 8:1).

The apostle Paul

Paul said: 'We are Christ's ambassadors' (2 Cor. 5:20), which is a
diplomatic (or irenic) concept, meaning that when he felt an interaction might not be productive, he might even withdraw from it (Acts
19:9,10). The other examples of Paul's interactions demonstrated a
'bold' side to his personality (2 Cor. 10:1), which surfaced both inside
and outside the church (v. 2).

Confronting insiders

When interacting with the Christian community, Paul used confrontational terminology as a metaphor for spiritual realities. For example, *military* terminology was used to refer to the *struggle* against
dark forces (Eph. 6:12): the 'weapons we *fight* with are not . . . of
[this] world' (2 Cor. 10:4), and the metaphor of armour portrays
the 'supernatural covering' of the truth of Christ (Eph. 6:10–16).
He also taught about the internal *battle* with human nature (1 Tim.
6:12), as well as a mental confrontation requiring invisible *weapons*
to overcome worldly lines of thinking (i.e. ideologies); these are to be

demolished (2 Cor. 10:5) using thoughts and words, not brute force or violence. Paul was speaking here to the Corinthian congregation with which he was engaged in a confrontation with recalcitrant Christians, who should have known better (v. 6). His approach reflects a firm but loving leadership style, which should not be understood as a licence for 'heavy shepherding'.

Confronting outsiders

It is also clear that Paul's 'boldness' was exhibited in the public sphere among unbelievers who might have been adherents of all sorts of ideologies. He and his team often confronted people and sought to 'demolish arguments'. They did so among Jews and Greek proselytes to Judaism because these groups were either attacking or deviating from the gospel.

Paul *reasons* with pagans in the marketplaces, urging them to change their allegiance to Christ (Acts 17:17) while seeking to *persuade* others to change religion (Acts 18:13); this is something frowned on by PC rules. Paul's team also engages people via 'signs and wonders' such as exorcism or healing (Acts 19:13–20), and also via *bold* and *persuasive* argument (Acts 19:8–9). However, he regularly sparked strong reactions, especially when he upset vested commercial interests (the human angle) or triggered the abandonment of other religions (the spiritual and political angle). Whatever style Paul and his team used, the assumption appeared to be that confrontation can create an *entrée* for the message (Acts 17:1–2,16–34).

Paul said metaphorically of one encounter: 'I *fought* with wild beasts in Ephesus' (1 Cor. 15:32). While scholars scrutinize this figurative language, it is clear that Paul was not intimidated even by 'ferocious' anger; on the contrary, he had to be restrained from wading back into the fray to press his case in a highly adversarial atmosphere. This incident became a talked-about spectacle that turbocharged Paul's message across that region (Acts 19:19,24–41). Paul received death threats, was thrown out of synagogues, sparked riots and was jailed for his own safety. This is unlikely to have been the case unless he was prepared to be confrontational.

An Apostolic Maxim for All Styles of Interaction

We have alluded to the fact that Jesus set the bar of interaction with 'grace and truth', whether the engagement was via conversation or dialogue or apologetics or confrontation. We could go further to say that this is arguably a tenet of the apostles' teaching (Acts 2:42). For example, the apostle James says: 'But the wisdom that comes from heaven is first of all pure [in motive and intention]; then peace-loving [non-aggressive and fostering ongoing relationships]' (Jas 3:17). The apostle Paul gives the following guidelines:

1. 'To the Jews I became like a Jew, to win the Jews. To those under the law [i.e. Torah/sharia] I became like one under the law . . . so that by *all possible means* I might save some' (1 Cor. 9:20–22). Is our attitude and action worthy of inclusion in the 'all possible means'?
2. Although we 'have the right to do *anything* . . . not everything is beneficial . . . [or] constructive' (1 Cor. 10:23). Is our attitude and action part of the 'anything', or is it part of the 'not beneficial'?
3. The fate of those who are abusive to us is 'destruction'; their 'god is . . . [their worldly appetite . . . their vanity]'; their 'glory is in their shame'; they 'focus their mind on earthly and temporal things' (Phil. 3:19 AMP). Does my attitude and action qualify for a place on this list?
4. 'Avoid foolish controversies and genealogies and arguments and quarrels about the law, because these are unprofitable and useless' (Titus 3:9). Just because the other participant wants to go off at a tangent does not mean we should comply.
5. 'Do not grieve the Holy Spirit of God, with whom you were sealed for the day of redemption. Get rid of all bitterness, rage and anger, brawling and slander, along with every form of malice. Be kind and compassionate to one another, forgiving each other, just as in

Christ God forgave you' (Eph. 4:30–32). If this is the bar set for interaction with fellow Christians, how can it be any lower with atheists, white supremacists or assertive people of other faiths?

This balance is supported in a helpful resource booklet which has been published to guide active Christians in their interaction in a secular and PC climate. *Speak Up: The Law and Your Gospel Freedoms* (2016) is a document that was devised by the Lawyers' Christian Fellowship for the Evangelical Alliance and offers biblical guidance on public debate as protected within the English legal system. The circuit judge David Turner QC describes this document as 'a lively and legally informed route map for courteous and competent Christian contention'.[16]

The four interactive styles are key, because they help us keep a balance. One Christian worker who has in-depth experience of life in one of the more volatile parts of the Muslim world put it like this in a personal email in October 2020:

> For me the issue is about *balance*. Far too often we try to knock holes in the other guy's beliefs, as if we can win people by knocking down everything they believe in. On the other extreme is the desire to promote peace at all costs and although Jesus is the Prince of Peace, peacemaking is not . . . the main objective of the gospel. The *balance* lies somewhere between the two poles. Think how confident Jesus was in expressing truth, and how winsome as crowds flocked to hear what he had to say. Ideally, we shouldn't have to choose one over the other; it's a tricky *balance*.

If the four styles complement and enrich one another, it is time to stop championing one *over* the rest, and start seeing that they all have a part to play. This has the potential to improve Christians' interaction with one another, as well as with Muslims. In this way, the 'rough ground' of Mount Mission can begin to be made 'smooth' (Isa. 40:4 NKJV). As this happens, we find ourselves standing at the entrance to Grace Pass, which is our destination. What is it? What are the implications of it? And what could the future look like as the mountain blockages begin to be navigated?

10

Grace Pass

The principle of 'grace and truth' in public discourse

Jesus said: 'If you have faith and . . . you say to this mountain, "Be removed and be cast into the sea," it will be done.'

Matt. 21:21 NKJV

In this chapter we explore the legacy of the 'Christ event' (i.e. the life, death and resurrection of Jesus Christ) and how his example of courteous attitude and actions effectively blasts a way through the mountain blockages that society faces today. We see how Christ *is* the way through the social landmines, and why he is a sure foundation for the construction of a better society at the corporate level as individuals follow his lead.

The academic and social commentator Professor Jordan Peterson had a dream in which he was standing in the graveyard of an old cathedral. In his dream, the graves started to open and great warrior kings of history stood up on their graves. They were all armed and, when they saw one another, began fighting among themselves. Suddenly they all stopped fighting and bowed down to the figure of Jesus Christ; then Peterson woke up.[1]

When Peterson reflected on the meaning of the dream, it occurred to him that if you took the most king-like quality of each king, and rolled them all into one essence, it would be symbolized best by Jesus Christ (the 'King of Kings', Rev. 19:16), the most 'transcendent embodied good' in human history. As a psychologist, Peterson suggests that even someone with tyrannical power feels the need to achieve the sort of embodied influence with which Christ inspires people to a unifying cause, which is a psychological, sociological and spiritual need in humankind. Peterson goes further to affirm this instinctive capacity to recognize the 'transcendent good' as a trait of the divine within humanity. It is this which gets translated as the so-called 'common good' of society. Human nature corrupts this when it falls into the hands of the leaders of totalitarianism regimes, but it remains centrally embedded in the Judeo-Christian heritage. In spite of the influence of an institutionalized form of Christianity, this heritage still carries within it the 'transcendent embodied good' in the person of Jesus Christ himself.

Although Peterson is speaking as a *non-religious* academic, his dream is a parable which describes the impact of 'Grace Pass' on society's seven mountain blockages. The conclusion of this conversation is as follows:

- Some key blockages exist in society, as described earlier, including 'Mount Imperial' (lingering colonialist assumptions), 'Mount Hegemony' (political and economic dominance), 'Mount Ethnos' (a racial pecking order), 'Mount Correct' (politically correct control), 'Mount Strident' (nationalist assumptions), 'Mount Occlusion' (Muslim defection) and 'Mount Mission' (Christians and Muslims disagreeing disagreeably among themselves).
- These blockages are leaking toxic waste into our attitudes and actions in an era that is now post-Christendom, post-colonial and multicultural (NB: *minorities* are no longer just racial but also religious, ideological and sexual).
- The guiding principles of the Judeo-Christian heritage offer a common platform for public discourse that can deliver social cohesion.
- The key players are the social minorities, but special responsibility is placed on the adherents of the Abrahamic faiths – Jews,

Christians and Muslims – who ought to model the *best* of what their tradition offers to achieve *good* interaction.

- Grace Pass is the route via which we can navigate social blockages and PC landmines. You may find this to be a curious expression, but it is a reference to the 'transcendent embodied good' in Jordan Peterson's dream. The 'good' is rooted in the person of Jesus Christ.

'Grace and Truth' – the Example of Jesus Christ

The way to the 'transcendent good' is the principle of 'grace and truth' (John 1:14,17), which is a balance of a 'gracious' attitude and faithfulness to 'truth'. These two are like two bookends which form the parameters of civilized behaviour: on the one hand is courteousness, and on the other hand is honesty, which enables us to face facts without fuelling fear. Jesus modelled this balance consistently, particularly when interacting with people who were thought by society to be 'other', such as racial, social or religious *minorities*.

Take, for instance, the Samaritan people, who in Jesus' day were the largest settled immigrant minority in his country, like the ethnic minorities of our day. Samaritans still exist in the modern Middle East and can trace their roots back to Iraq (2 Kgs 17:24–34), yet all mentions of them seem to be negative (Neh. 2:19; John 4:9), which is why in the Israel of Jesus' time, Samaritans were racially abused, politically suspect and socially marginalized. Their beliefs were a hybrid of Judaism and some pagan elements. Jews could be hostile to them, yet Jesus' interaction with them was always courteous and calm, and had a personable tone. Jesus' lone interaction with the socially isolated Samaritan woman at the well in Sychar (John 4) was a master class in 'grace and truth', where in one conversation the woman transitioned from disdain ('you are a *Jew*', v. 9), to politeness ('Sir', v. 11), to respect ('I can see that you are a prophet', v. 19), to reverence ('Could this be the Messiah?', v. 29).

Jesus also helped his followers to see Samaritan people not as a 'stumbling-block' but as a 'stepping-stone' to other racial groups, which the apostle Paul later called those in 'the regions beyond' (2 Cor. 10:16). Jesus was never aggressive or nasty to Samaritans; quite the opposite, he created the parable of the Good Samaritan, who was the hero of the story (John 10). Luke also makes clear that it was a Samaritan leprosy sufferer who had the courtesy to return to *thank* Jesus for a healing (Luke 17:11–19). Jesus even gave Samaria its own mention in the Great Commission (Acts 1:8; 8:14), which suggests a category of people who are 'other' but also *close* – perhaps *too* close for comfort.

Jesus was active in the most multicultural region of Israel in his day: 'Galilee of the *nations*' (Isa. 9:1; Matt. 4:15). This would include Syrians, Italians, Lebanese, Palestinians and Greeks, as well as the Samaritans mentioned above. If Jesus is the example, the fulfilling of his Great Commission is also to be motivated by 'grace and truth', which means a holistic (i.e. whole-life) engagement with others, as follows:

1. *work* (i.e. love/grace encounter) – via practical service, helping, alleviating suffering at the point of felt need
2. *wonder* (i.e. power/supernatural encounter) – via healing prayer, deliverance from the demonic
3. *word* (i.e. truth/cerebral encounter) – via explanations of what was happening, why, and what it meant.

My own reading of the Gospels leads me to think Jesus emphasized these in this order, yet western evangelical Christians tend to reverse the order to give primacy to 'word' (i.e. verbal proclamation) and even deleting 'wonders' from the list altogether (perhaps leaving that to Pentecostals).

The notion of 'whole-life engagement' is a rabbinic pattern of getting to know people well enough to have a mutually nurturing relationship with them, which is a far cry from the modern propagandist understanding of 'evangelism'. Whole-life engagement is more likely to be what Jesus had in mind when he said: 'Make disciples [among] all nations' (Matt. 28:19). This is a mentoring lifestyle rather than a gospel formula.

'Grace and Truth' in Secular Discourse

We must say here that 'grace and truth' is a universal *principle*, which means it has an application in all spheres of national life.

For active Christians, it is a manifestation of the kingdom of God, and they would describe it as providing the needed constraint on human nature in order to maintain healthy interaction. In the words of the apostle Paul: 'The love of Christ constrains us' (2 Cor. 5:14 WEB), which evokes the picture of our attitude and actions being constrained by 'grace and truth' in the same way that the banks of a swollen river are a constraint to the water and prevent a messy overflow.

In a non-faith context, 'grace and truth' was modelled by people such as Mahatma Gandhi, Martin Luther King Jr and Nelson Mandela. They were all committed to accurate *facts* (i.e. truth) but without vitriol or a violent reaction to an opposing argument or those making it (i.e. grace).

'Grace and Truth' in Christian/Muslim Discourse

We said earlier that the Qur'an is framed in 'polemic' terms, which is why it is more natural for ardent Muslims to interact in a polemic or adversarial way. This raises the question of what is *appropriate* in our style and tone to ensure that our interactions help social cohesion rather than hinder it. It is a safeguard when we approach the 'other' with an attitude that is *conciliatory* rather than *crusading* and *coercive* (i.e. imposing a truth claim on the other participant). The 'grace and truth' principle seeks to enter into the other person's world rather than *impose* our own on them.[2] It crosses the boundaries between us rather than crushing the boundary.[3]

The apostle John knew Jesus well and described him as the one who is '*full* of grace and truth' (John 1:14). If Jesus were to have a social media account today, I suspect it might well be called something like #grace&truth. As an expression, 'grace and truth' is loaded with the concept of incarnation or 'enfleshment', because Christ the divine entered human experience (John 1:14a). This is arguably the most stunning act of divine grace in human history. Jesus also 'made his home *among* us' by coming to live in 'proximity' to us (see John 1:14b). John also says that Jesus 'made the Father known' (see John 1:18). This was by *being* good news as well as *talking* about it.

Impacts of 'Grace and Truth'

Some Christian friends of mine in the East End of London discovered that 'grace' earths 'truth' in the same way that a lightning rod earths lightning. Their next-door neighbours were Muslims who, after being on the receiving end of some random acts of kindness, asked them: 'Why do you love us so much?', which opened the way to *tell* them why. The Christians were heard because the Muslims knew the words were real (true) and motivated by love (grace). My friends have asked why they got this response, and my answer would be: 'Because you live in Grace Pass'.

Another friend of mine moved home, and his Muslim neighbour hugged him and wept openly on the street, asking: 'Where will I ever find such a godly neighbour like you?' A similar thing happened to me when the security services in Egypt asked me to leave the country. A Muslim friend said to me: 'You are the best Muslim I have ever known – and yet you're a Christian!' I wonder what he was seeing that prompted that?

The whole-life engagement of 'grace and truth' can be problematic for some evangelicals who see verbal proclamation as the *only* way that is biblically valid in Christian interaction, rather than a non-negotiable component of it. The 'grace and truth' principle in Christian witness is a blend of the 'Great *Command* of Christ' to *love* our neighbour,[4] and the 'Great *Commission* of Christ' to *tell* our neighbour.[5] The two operate like parallel railway tracks. Bishop Tom Wright reportedly said: 'The apostle John said the word became flesh, but we are in danger of turning the flesh back into word.' The incarnation of Jesus shows it is not enough to merely affirm truth cerebrally; truth is realized (i.e. made real) when we visibly live it out in our attitude and actions – as Jesus and disciples such as Stephen did. This got both men killed, and people are not usually killed for merely being 'nice' but for manifesting an alternative truth claim that is not always welcome. The 'grace and truth' principle is also an embodiment of the Beatitudes (i.e. the 'Beautiful Attitudes') of Jesus.[6] This means not just talking *about* good news but also *being* good news, which lifts the whole engagement above mere 'propaganda'.

The Lausanne Movement affirmed this when it chose the titles of two consecutive consultations. The first was: 'Let the earth *hear* his voice' (i.e. the verbal proclamation of 'truth'), and the next event was: 'May Muslims *feel* his touch' (i.e. truth lived out with 'grace').[7] This is a reminder that the truth about Jesus comes wrapped in the faulty human beings who are commending him. Such flawed followers of Jesus are needed more urgently now because the times are changing, and more Muslims are changing their heart allegiance to Jesus Christ than at any time in history. It is as if a divine sonic whistle is reverberating in the hearts of enquiring Muslims everywhere, drawing them to the Messiah (John 12:32). They are 'sheep from *another* sheepfold' (see John 10:16) who are hearing the call to 'come home'! More on this in a moment.

Mountains Can, and Do, Move

Our conclusion is that mountains *can* and *do* move (Matt. 21:21). This is what explains historic shifts such as the abolition of slavery, the emancipation of women, the overthrow of fascism in Italy and Spain, the fall of the Berlin Wall with the dissolution of the communist bloc, the dismantling of apartheid in South Africa and the Arab

Spring. It is reassuring to know that the Almighty is the ultimate arbiter of human history: '[he] works out everything in conformity with the purpose of his will' (Eph. 1:11). God's purposes may move slowly, but they are sure and unstoppable. The British evangelist J. John impacted me by saying: 'There are two reasons why people don't accept Jesus; one is that they *don't* know a Christian, and the other is that they *do* know a Christian.'[8] In the first half of the twenty-first century, the world is witnessing turbulent and painful change, but are we going to be a help or a hindrance? Active Christians can play a crucial role by acting like 'spiritual midwives' for all those who are navigating their way through the mountain blockages to Grace Pass.

In chapter 8 we mentioned the prophetic observation of Bishop Kenneth Cragg, who foresaw the day when the house of Islam would have to choose between the 'Medinan priority' (i.e. an orientation of power, control and exclusion) and the 'Meccan priority' (i.e. an orientation of vulnerability, flexibility and inclusion). His words are coming to pass in our day when there is a growing awareness of the human right to choose our allegiances, and the freedom to act on those choices without reprisals.

The Meccan priority is the stuff of the reform process we have already described, which to my mind is part of the slow process of the 'redemption of the house of Islam'. The sketchy image of Christ within the Qur'an becomes the stepping-stone to further information about Jesus in the Bible, and so a personal transaction is taking place: 'whenever anyone turns to the Lord, the veil is taken away' (2 Cor. 3:16).

It is all too easy to remain an armchair critic who is obsessed with the 'signs of the times' while failing to discern the 'need of the hour'. Our Christian counterparts in the early church did the same when Gentile 'outsiders' began finding their way to Jesus Christ and seeking to attach themselves to a community of Christ-followers (i.e. a church). As Gentile newcomers attached to the Jewish church they were not rejoiced over very much, nor were they received well. Instead, they were required to jump through hoops which were more cultural than doctrinally necessary. This prompted a special meeting, the 'Council of Jerusalem', which concluded that 'no *unnecessary* burden' should be put on newcomers from other ethnic, cultural or religious backgrounds (see Acts 15). It is ironic that within two centuries, the church became mainly non-Jewish. To serve today's newcomers with a tangible connection to the good news about Jesus is not just an act of Christian witness; it has now become a 'civic duty' as well. My recommended read on this issue is *Distinctively Welcoming* by Revd Dr Richard Sudworth.[9] However, what about those who do not even know they are spiritually homeless?

Grace Pass Leads 'Home'

Although what we have been saying also applies to all minorities in society, including sexual minorities, I keep defaulting to the needs of Muslims for reasons made clear in chapter 1. In the light of all the above chapters, we can see that a significant number of people with a Muslim family background now find themselves in the West, where some may feel socially disengaged. For a minority of these, it is worse because they feel caught between a white 'host' culture on the one hand, and the notion of a non-terrestrial Islamic State on the other. This creates a sense of rootlessness and a search for belonging and meaning, as identified by the analyst Jenny Taylor who describes this dilemma using the vision of 'home',[10] as captured in T.S. Eliot's poem 'Little Gidding'.[11] The poem resonates with an invitation to the kingdom of God, where society no longer needs to categorize anyone by human characteristics such as their race, gender, religion or culture. Like the kingdom of God, 'home' is spiritual and yet real; it is coming and yet it has arrived; it is here and yet it is nowhere; it is never and yet it is always. Taylor goes on to describe the followers of Jesus Christ as a 'storied' people, a 'pilgrim' people – 'roamers' who do not roam aimlessly, because they are going somewhere. All social interaction becomes part of a 'recovery process' in the narrative of *homecoming* to the Father, in whose house there are 'many rooms' (John 14:2).

I personally live (and am prepared to die) for the day when the words of the prophet Isaiah come to pass: 'every mountain and hill *will* be made low' (see Isa. 40:4). I am believing for the redemption of the house of Islam, and we have seen some of the more observable indicators. I am also believing for what seems to be the greater challenge of our day, namely an end to the negative narrative about Muslims that gets thrown over *all* Muslims like a wet blanket. That sentiment falls short of the benchmark set by the apostle Paul where love 'bears all things, believes all things, hopes all things, endures all things'. In the same passage the apostle also says: 'Love suffers long and is kind . . . does not behave rudely . . . is not [easily] provoked, thinks no evil . . . rejoices in the truth' (1 Cor. 13:4–7 NKJV).

I long for the negative cynicism in western culture to be dampened down, and for the squabbles among active Christians to give way to the day when 'the glory of the LORD will be revealed, and *all* people will see it together' (Isa. 40:5). Our mountainous social blockages are littered with the toxic rubble deposited by historic events, past, recent and present. The way forward involves helping mountains to move, as the feet of *all* of us become 'beautiful on the mountains' like hinds' feet in *high* places (Isa. 52:7; Ps. 18:33), rather than a clumsy 'bull in a china shop'. For me, full social cohesion is only found via Grace Pass.

Notes

1: And the Problem Is . . .

[1] All emphasis in Scripture quotations is mine.

[2] S. Bell, *Grace for Muslims? The Journey from Fear to Faith* (Milton Keynes: Authentic, 2006).

[3] In Orthodox Judaism and Islam, physical and spiritual defilement go together and are treated like an infection that must be cleansed by prescribed rituals. See more in my book *Gospel for Muslims: Learning to Read the Bible through Eastern Eyes* (Milton Keynes: Authentic, 2012), pp. 160–67.

[4] B. Lewis, *The Crisis of Islam: Holy War and Unholy Terror* (London: Phoenix, 2003), p. 4.

[5] 'Hamza Trial: Evidence on Day One', BBC News (11 January 2006) http://news.bbc.co.uk/1/hi/uk/4603370.stm (accessed 10 July 2020).

[6] I. Shah, *Elephant in the Dark* (Bath: ISF, 2016).

[7] 'Blind Men and an Elephant', Wikipedia, https://en.wikipedia.org/wiki/Blind_men_and_an_elephant (accessed 7 Sept. 2020).

[8] 'House of Islam' is *dar ul-Islam* in Arabic. It means all who belong within the global community of Muslims. The term was first used in the Bible, e.g. the 'house of Jacob' or the 'house of Israel' (see Obad. 1:18 NKJV).

2: The Right to Write

[1] *The Today Programme*, Radio 4, 9 March 2020.

[2] J. Humphrys, 'My Wake-Up Call to the Woke BBC', *Daily Mail*, 5 September 2020, pp. 20–21.

3   W. Brueggemann, 'Mrs. Thompson's Call for Honest Grief', blog, Church Anew (18 June 2020) https://churchanew.org/brueggemann/walter-brueggemann/mrs-thompsons-call-for-honest-grief?rq=thompson (accessed 7 Sept. 2020).

4   X. Fonseca, S. Lukosch and F. Brazier, 'Social Cohesion Revisited: A New Definition and How to Characterize It', Taylor & Francis Online (16 July 2018) https://www.tandfonline.com/doi/full/10.1080/13511610.2018.1497480 (accessed 7 Sept. 2020).

5   J. Wynne-Jones, 'Bishop Warns of No-Go Zones for Non-Muslims', *The Telegraph* (6 January 2008) https://www.telegraph.co.uk/news/uknews/1574694/Bishop-warns-of-no-go-zones-for-non-Muslims.html (accessed 8 June 2020).

6   S. Bell, 'I Have a Dream', postlude in *Grace for Muslims? The Journey from Fear to Faith* (Milton Keynes: Authentic, 2006), pp. 181–5.

7   *30 Days of Prayer: Muslim World Prayer Guide*, https://www.30daysprayer.com (accessed 7 Sept. 2020).

8   The petition in Muslim prayer is 'Lead us in the right path' (*sirat ul-mustaqeem*), Qur'an, Surah Al-Fatiha.

3: Mount Imperial

1   J. Ingleby, *Beyond Empire: Postcolonialism and Mission in a Global Context* (Milton Keynes: Author House, 2010), pp. xvii–xviii.

2   Keele University, *Prof Dorling (Uni of Oxford) – Brexit and the End of the British Empire*, video, YouTube (20 May 2019) https://youtu.be/AM5-lhrztc4 (accessed 29 Dec. 2020).

3   Ingleby, *Beyond Empire*, p. 4.

4   Ingleby, *Beyond Empire*, p. 8.

5   P. Lewis, 'The Challenge Facing Muslim Communities in the UK: Between Alienation and Normalization', lecture, Birmingham, 27 November 2010.

6   Account by the ancient historian Eusebius, *Life of Constantine* 23; 4.62.

7   J. Lidstone, *Give Up the Purple: A Call for Servant Leadership in Hierarchical Cultures* (Carlisle: Langham Global Library, 2019), pp. 6–7. Lidstone also cites Alan Kreider, *The Patient Ferment of the Early Church: The Improbable Rise of Christianity in the Roman Empire* (Grand Rapids, MI: Baker, 2016).

8   Sabine Baring-Gould (1834–1924).

[9] T. Holland, *Dominion: The Making of the Western Mind* (London: Little Brown, 2019).

[10] K. Wilson, *Jesus Brand Spirituality: He Wants His Religion Back* (Nashville: Thomas Nelson, 2008), p. 3.

[11] Isaac Watts (1674–1748).

[12] E. Arthur, 'Throwback: Our Place in the World', blog, Kouyanet (19 March 2020) https://www.kouya.net/?s=throwback%3A+our+place+in+the+world.

[13] P. Weston, *Lesslie Newbigin: Missionary Theologian. A Reader* (London: SPCK, 2006), p. 185.

[14] Between 2001 and 2011 there has been a decrease in people who identify as Christian (from 71.7% to 59.3%) and an increase in those reporting no religion (from 14.8% to 25.1%). Office of National Statistics (2011) https://www.ons.gov.uk/census (accessed 7 Sept. 2020).

[15] J.I. Packer, *Knowing Christianity* (Wheaton, IL: Harold Shaw, 1995), p. 60.

[16] D. Lawson, 'There Is a Moral Vacuum in Britain', *The Mail on Sunday*, 5 November 2006, p. 62.

[17] E. Durkheim, 'Elementary Forms of Religious Life', in *Sociology of Religion: Selected Readings* (ed. R. Robertson; Harmondsworth: Penguin, 1969), p. 48.

[18] A. Hastings, *The Construction of Nationhood: Ethnicity, Religion and Nationalism* (Cambridge: Cambridge University Press, 1997), p. 36.

[19] S. Bruce, *God Is Dead: Secularization in the West* (Oxford: Blackwell, 2002), p. 2.

[20] C. Morton, *Is God Still an Englishman? How We Lost Our Faith (But Found New Soul)* (London: Little Brown, 2010).

[21] G. Davie, *Religion in Britain since 1945* (Oxford: Blackwell, 1994), p. 14.

[22] Statement made on BBC TV chat show, *Have Your Say*; see 'Dawkins: I'm a Cultural Christian', BBC News (10 December 2007) http://news.bbc.co.uk/1/hi/uk_politics/7136682.stm (accessed 7 Sept. 2020).

[23] Unbelievable?, *NT Wright & Tom Holland – How St Paul Changed the World*, video, YouTube (20 July 2018) http://youtu.be/nlf_ULB26cU (accessed 2 May 2020).

[24] P.L. Berger, ed., *The Desecularization of the World: Resurgent Religion and World Politics* (Grand Rapids, MI: Eerdmans, 1999), pp. 2–3.

[25] Bruce, *God Is Dead*, p. 199.

[26] C. Jonathan, Commission on Religion and Belief in British Public Life (CORAB), January 2016.

[27] Maranatha Community, a statement for a debate in the House of Commons, 27 January 2015, www.maranathacommunity.org.uk.

[28] Rageh Omaar was educated at the Dragon Preparatory School, Cheltenham College and New College Oxford.

[29] R. Omaar, *Only Half of Me: Being a Muslim in Britain* (London: Viking, 2006), pp. 28–30.

4: Mount Hegemony

[1] The American political activist and commentator.

[2] ἡγεμονία, *hēgemonía*.

[3] *Noughts & Crosses*, a TV drama series based on the novels of Malorie Blackman and aired on BBC 1, March 2020.

[4] Cited in the two-part TV documentary *House of Saud: A Family at War*, BBC 2, January 2018.

[5] C.J.H. Wright, *These Are Your Gods: Faithful Discipleship in Idolatrous Times* (Leicester: IVP, 2020).

[6] 'Rule Britannia', lyrics by James Thomson (1740); music by Thomas Arne.

[7] E. Arthur, 'The Other Side of the Coin', blog, Kouyanet (1 September 2020) https://www.kouya.net/?p=11549 (accessed 29 Dec. 2020).

[8] Asif Gokak, *Dr Zakir Naik Conferred King Faisal International Prize by Saudi Arabia*, video (26 January 2018) https://youtu.be/prl16bwFwC0 (accessed 4 Feb. 2020).

[9] J. Pilger, *The New Rulers of the World* (London: Verso, 2002).

5: Mount Ethnos

[1] W.E.B. Du Bois, *The Souls of Black Folk* (Harlow: Longman, 2002 [1903]), p. 89.

[2] My own definition. See more at: https://www.bing.com/search?q=definition+of+racism&form=EDGHPT&qs=DA&cvid=49e12696fd3440d980cca2bd4df0309f&refig=5e60d1f26b0e4ef285e7cef5fe9f25a1&cc=GB&setlang=en (accessed 21 June 2020).

[3] T. Modood, 'Islamophobia: A Form of Cultural Racism', a submission to the All-Party Parliamentary Group on British Muslims, 1 June 2018.

[4] Rwanda, Tutsi/Hutu tribal conflict, https://www.thoughtco.com/history-of-hutu-tutsi,-conflict-3554917 (accessed 7 Sept. 2020).

5 Nigeria, Jukun/Tive tribal conflict, https://www.thenetnaija.com/forum/general/crime/38437-killed-jukun-tive-ethnic-groups-clash-benue-state (accessed 7 Sept. 2020).

6 *The Sunday Programme*, BBC Radio 4, 28 June 2020.

7 R.S. Reddie, *Black Muslims in Britain: Why Are a Growing Number of Young Black People Converting to Islam?* (Oxford: Lion Hudson, 2009), p. 149.

8 Reddie, *Black Muslims in Britain*, p. 151.

9 Reddie, *Black Muslims in Britain*, p. 213.

10 Reddie, *Black Muslims in Britain*, p. 151.

11 BRIC TV, *Imam of Harlem: On Being Black & Muslim in America*, video, YouTube (1 November 2017) https://www.youtube.com/watch?v=9lYK3MV9wuc&t=2s (accessed 27 July 2020).

12 The term 'Islamophobia' originally meant the 'fear', 'dislike' or 'hatred' of Muslims/Islam by non-Muslims as the 'natural and irreconcilable enemy of the Christian and the European . . . the negation of civilization . . . barbarism, bad faith and cruelty' – Alain Quellien (quoted in Z. Iqbal, *Islamophobia: History, Context and Deconstruction* [Thousand Oaks, CA: Sage, 2019], p. 42). The word first appeared in 1923 in an article by Jonas Otterbeck in the *Journal of Theological Studies* and entered general use in a report by the Runnymede Trust in 1997. First used in the political sphere by Kofi Annan, Secretary General of the United Nations, in December 2004, the term was later brought into common parlance by Trevor Phillips.

13 APPG on British Muslims, *Islamophobia Defined: The Inquiry into a Working Definition of Islamophobia/Anti-Muslim Hatred* (27 November 2018) https://appgbritishmuslims.org/publications (accessed 23 Jan. 2021).

14 'Islamophobia Definition "Unfit for Purpose", Say Campaigners', National Secular Society (15 May 2019) www.secularism.org.uk/news/2019/05/islamophobia-definition-unfit-for-purpose-say-campaigners (accessed 11 Aug. 2020).

15 'Killing of George Floyd', Wikipedia, https://en.wikipedia.org/wiki/Killing_of_George_Floyd (accessed 2 June 2020).

16 Prager U, *Black Lives Matter Is a Marxist Movement*, video, YouTube (1 July 2020) https://www.youtube.com/watch?v=rpLItQnrgec (accessed 23 Jan. 2021).

17 G. Adams, 'Black Lives Matter: Anarchist Manifesto', *Daily Mail*, 20 June 2020, pp. 10–11.

18 BBC 1 News, 8 June 2020.

19 D. Gordon, director, *The Australian Dream*, TV documentary, BBC 2, 9 August 2020.

20 The Real Hidden Colors of Slavery, *Ghanaian Author Speaks on How the Arab Slave Trade Has Been Ignored and Romanticized*, video, interview with Dr. J.A. Azumah on his book *The Legacy of Arab-Islam in Africa* (Oxford: Oneworld, 2004), YouTube (31 July 2015) https://youtu.be/hV-KAyW7pI8 (accessed 1 July 2020).

21 Thomas Sowell, Senior Fellow at the Hoover Institution, Stanford University, 'The Scapegoat for Strife in the Black Community', *National Review* (7 July 2015) https://www.nationalreview.com/2015/07/slavery-didnt-cause-todays-black-problems-welfare-did (accessed 29 June 2020).

22 Sowell, 'The Scapegoat for Strife in the Black Community'.

23 D. Shaw, *The Today Programme*, BBC Radio 4, 30 June 2020, citing an unpublished Home Office report seen by the BBC.

24 *The Rasmussen Report*, 7 March 2013.

25 Oxford Union, *Donald Mayfield Brown – the United States Is Institutionally Racist*, video, YouTube (12 May 2015) https://www.youtube.com/watch?v=yuyClLZpeKk (accessed 24 Jan. 2021).

26 Oxford Union, *David Webb – the United States Is Not Institutionally Racist*, video, YouTube (12 May 2015) https://www.youtube.com/watch?v=pv7hsiUirUU (accessed 24 Jan. 2021).

27 G. Joo, 'Unmasking Racism, Starting with Me', Gospel Coalition (6 June 2020) www.thegospelcoalition.org/article/unmasking-racism-starting-with-me (accessed 2 Feb. 2020).

28 The Rubin Report, *The Myth of Systemic Racism (Pt 2)*, video, interview with Coleman Hughes, YouTube (11 October 2018) https://youtu.be/1sV5qU6e-YY (accessed 29 May 2020).

29 The Rubin Report, *Conservatives, Black Lives Matter, Racism*, video, interview with Larry Elder, YouTube (15 January 2016) https://youtu.be/IFqVNPwsLNo (accessed 10 June 2020).

30 *Race Disparity Audit: Summary Findings from the Ethnicity Facts and Figures Website* (London: Cabinet Office, October 2017; rev. 2018) https://www.gov.uk/government/publications/race-disparity-audit.

31 K. Iqbal, *Dear Birmingham: A Conversation with My Hometown* (London: Xlibris, 2013).

32 See A. Wheatle, 'I Spent Four Months in Prison', *The Telegraph Magazine*, 28 March 2020, p. 66.

33 D. Shaw, 'Stephen Lawrence: How Has His Murder Changed Policing?', BBC News (19 February 2019) https://www.bbc.com/news/uk-47161480 (accessed 7 Sept. 2020); J. Halliday, 'Met Chief Admits

Institutional Racism Claims Have "Some Justification"', *The Guardian* (5 June 2015) https://www.theguardian.com/uk-news/2015/jun/05/met-chief-admits-institutional-racism-claims-have-some-justification (accessed 7 Sept. 2020).

34 J. Moir, interview with Emma Thynn, Viscountess Weymouth, poised to be Britain's first black marchioness: 'I Pray for the Day When My Race Is *Strictly* Not an Issue', *Daily Mail*, 7 September 2019, pp. 26–7.

35 A.T. Nwaubani, 'Eton College: Nigerian Author Recalls Racist Abuse', BBC News (22 June 2020), https://www.bbc.co.uk/news/amp/world-africa-53062502 (accessed 24 June 2020).

36 L. Winket, Rector of St James' Piccadilly, *Thought for the Day*, Radio 4, 20 November 2019.

37 'General Synod Votes to Apologise over Racism', The Church of England (11 February 2020) https://www.churchofengland.org/news-and-media/news-and-statements/general-synod-votes-apologise-over-racism (accessed 24 Jan. 2021).

38 'Black Trainee Vicar Rejected from Curacy Post Critical of Apology', *Christian Today* (20 June 2020) https://www.christiantoday.com/article/black.trainee.vicar.rejected.from.curacy.post.critical.of.apology/135062.htm (accessed 25 June 2020).

39 Ipsos Mori poll on racial integration, cited in 'Black Lives Matter: "Much More That We Need to Do" to Tackle Racism – PM', BBC News (15 June 2020) https://www.bbc.co.uk/news/uk-53045349 (accessed 7 Sept. 2020).

40 *Black Lives Matter: Rivers of Blood 50 Years On*, TV documentary, Channel 5, 3 June 2020.

41 An organization working for equality and inclusion in English football is Kick It Out, https://www.kickitout.org (accessed 25 June 2020).

42 'Racism and Racial Bullying', Childline, https://www.childline.org.uk/info-advice/bullying-abuse-safety/crime-law/racism-racial-bullying (accessed 21 June 2020).

43 'Racist Incident Filmed on Ryanair Flight – Video' (source: Facebook/David Lawrence), *The Guardian* (21 October 2018) https://www.theguardian.com/world/video/2018/oct/21/racist-incident-filmed-on-ryanair-flight-video (accessed 21 June 2020).

44 *The Russell Howard Hour*, series 1, episode 1, Sky One TV, 12 July 2017.

45 G. Fraser, 'How Cancel Culture Makes Liars of Us All', *The Post*, UnHerd (11 June 2020) www.unherd.com/2020/06/how-cancel-culture-makes-liars-of-us-all (accessed 24 Jan. 2021).

46 Fraser, 'How Cancel Culture Makes Liars of Us All.'

6: Mount Correct

1 'Political Correctness', Wikipedia, https://en.wikipedia.org/wiki/Political_correctness (accessed 29 Dec. 2020).

2 M. Foucault, *The History of Sexuality: vol. 1: An Introduction* (trans. R. Hurley; New York: Pantheon, 1978), p. 94.

3 LAD, *Jordan Peterson – Political Correctness – Oxford Union*, video, YouTube (26 November 2018) https://www.youtube.com/watch?v=uUKlvO_h7Hs (accessed 5 Sept. 2020).

4 J.K. Rowling 'cancelled': I. Lewis, 'JK Rowling Trans Row: What Have Emma Watson, Daniel Radcliffe and Rupert Grint Said in Response?', *Independent* (12 June 2020) https://www.independent.co.uk/arts-entertainment/books/news/jk-rowling-trans-harry-potter-rupert-grint-daniel-racliffe-emma-watson-bonnie-wright-a9560376.html (accessed 27 July 2020).

5 W. Pavia, 'Author Faces Threats after She Warns of Trans Epidemic', *The Times*, 21 November 2020, p. 47.

6 The Christian Institute, *The Transgender Craze* (September 2020) www.christian.org.uk/transgendercraze-ref.

7 A. 'Dotty' Charles, *Outraged: Why Everyone Is Shouting and No One Is Talking* (London: Bloomsbury, 2020); comments reported in A. Charles, 'Black, Gay and Outspoken', *Times Magazine*, 3 July 2020, p. 10.

8 Real Time with Bill Maher, *Jordan B. Peterson*, video, YouTube (21 April 2018) https://youtu.be/8wLCmDtCDAM (accessed 5 Aug. 2020).

9 The Telegraph, *Lawrence Fox in Racism Row over Meghan Markle on Question Time*, video, YouTube (17 January 2020) https://www.youtube.com/watch?v=_jhQsp4Ow0A (accessed 5 Sept. 2020).

10 Snaves, *10 Comedians on Political Correctness*, video, YouTube (20 January 2019) https://youtu.be/pLifGCKfLPQ (accessed 21 June 2020).

11 *10 Comedians on Political Correctness*, Stephen Fry comment.

12 J. McDowell and B. Hostetler, *The New Tolerance* (Wheaton, IL: Tyndale House, 1998), p. 42.

13 J. Petre, 'Leave Christmas Alone, Say Muslims', *The Telegraph*, 13 November 2006.

14 The local authorities I was made aware of at the time included Waltham Forest, London, and the cities of Birmingham and Preston City which balanced this with a suggestion that churches ring their bells at Easter.

15 M. Hasan, 'Jesus: the Muslim Prophet', *New Statesman* (10 December 2009) https://www.newstatesman.com/religion/2009/12/jesus-islam-muslims-prophet (accessed 5 Feb. 2021).

16 N. Afzal, 'No More Hiding from the Truth about Covid', *Daily Mail*, 1 August 2020, pp. 18–19.

17 Afzal, 'No More Hiding', p. 7.

18 I. Paul, 'Why Is Franklin Graham Being Turned Away?', Psephizo (30 January 2020) https://www.psephizo.com/life-ministry/why-is-franklin-graham-being-turned-away (accessed 7 Sept. 2020).

19 Dr J. Smith in a newsletter, December 2019; see also his online work, PfanderFilms, YouTube, https://www.youtube.com/user/PfanderFilms/videos (accessed 7 Sept. 2020).

20 D. Wood, *YouTube Declares War on Christians*, video, YouTube, https://youtu.be/8vGm3071XJk (accessed 6 June 2020 but taken down by YouTube); also D. Wood, *Understanding Trump's Executive Order on Preventing Online Censorship*, video, YouTube (3 June 2020) https://www.youtube.com/watch?v=rnI-5hJcIB0 (accessed 21 June 2020).

21 E. Shaw, *The Plausibility Problem: The Church and Same-Sex Attraction* (Leicester: IVP, 2015). For the case in support of SSA Christian celibacy, see Living Out, https://www.livingout.org (accessed 7 Sept. 2020).

22 M. Vines, *God and the Gay Christian: The Biblical Case in Support of Same-Sex Relationships* (New York: Convergent, 2014); also V. Beeching, *Undivided: Coming Out, Becoming Whole and Living Free from Shame* (London: William Collins, 2018). For the case in support of SSA Christians in faithful same-sex relationships, see Reformation Project, https://reformationproject.org (accessed 29 July 2020).

23 ONS survey in 2018: 7.9% of the UK population identify themselves as 'same-sex attracted', i.e. 1.2% in Northern Ireland, 2.0% in Scotland, 2.4% in Wales, 2.3% in England, https://www.ons.gov.uk/peoplepopulationandcommunity/culturalidentity (accessed 22 Aug. 2020).

24 T. Prill, 'Mission – Quo Vadis? The Current Theological Crisis in Evangelical Mission Organizations', *Evangelicals Now*, August 2012, p. 18.

25 Avi Yemini, *This Is the Only BLM Protest Video You Need to See*, video, YouTube (7 June 2020) https://youtu.be/tm86QPhCwFc (accessed 1 Aug. 2020).

26 Dr David Starkey in F. Phillips, '"Gay and Atheist" David Starkey Is Defending Christian Conscience More Clearly Than Our Bishops', *Catholic Herald* (10 March 2011) https://catholicherald.co.uk/gay-and-atheist-david-starkey-is-defending-christian-conscience-more-clearly-than-our-bishops (accessed 7 Sept. 2020).

27 M. Accad, 'Sacred Misinterpretation across the Christian-Muslim Divide', *International Journal of Frontier Missiology* 36.4 (Winter 2019): pp. 173–8.

7: Mount Strident

[1] Saying attributed to her 'priest friend Tom' in A. Lamott, *Bird by Bird* (New York: Pantheon, 1994), p. 22; https://writingshed.me/2010/04/17/when-god-hates-the-same-people-you-do.

[2] L. Dearden (citing Home Office figures), 'Religious Hate Crime Rises 40% in England and Wales – with More Than Half Directed at Muslims', *Independent* (16 October 2018) https://www.independent.co.uk/news/uk/crime/uk-hate-crime-religious-muslims-islamophobia-police-racism-a8585846.html (accessed 21 June 2020).

[3] N. Morley, 'Hate Crimes against Jewish People in the UK Rise to Record Levels', *Metro News* (2 February 2017) https://metro.co.uk/2017/02/02/hate-crimes-against-jewish-people-in-the-uk-rise-to-record-levels-6421974 (accessed 7 Sept. 2020).

[4] D.J. Philip, 'Twitter to Crackdown on Racist Abuse of Black Footballers', *The Voice* (22 August 2019) https://www.voice-online.co.uk/article/twitter-crackdown-racist-abuse-black-footballers (accessed 7 Sept. 2020).

[5] Abuse of MPs has doubled since 2017: M. Beckford, 'MPs under Threat: Abuse and Threats Aimed at MPs Has Hit Record Levels, Warn Police Chiefs', *The Sun* (8 May 2019) https://www.thesun.co.uk/news/9033641/mps-abuse-threats-record-level (accessed 7 Sept. 2020).

[6] Abuse of the police is running at 72 incidents a day or 1 every 20 minutes in England and Wales: 'Rise in Attacks on Police, as Officers Forced to Respond to Crimes Alone', *The Telegraph* (12 August 2018) www.telegraph.co.uk/news/2018/08/12/rise-attacks-police-officers-forced-respond-crimes-alone (accessed 7 Sept. 2020).

[7] M. Bulman, 'Attacks on LGBT Surge Almost 80% in UK over Last Four Years', *Independent* (7 September 2017) https://www.independent.co.uk/news/uk/home-news/gay-lgbt-hate-crimes-stats-rise-four-year-physical-verbal-homophobic-abuse-community-a7933126.html (accessed 25 Jan. 2021).

[8] D. Goodhart, *The Road to Somewhere: The New Tribes Shaping British Politics* (London: Penguin, 2017).

[9] 'New Process Set Out to Establish a Working Definition of Islamophobia', Gov.UK (16 May 2019) https://www.gov.uk/government/news/new-process-set-out-to-establish-a-working-definition-of-islamophobia.

[10] B. White, 'Discerning Facts from the Fears', a paper given at a day conference, 'The Numbers Game: Britain's Changing Demographics and the Implication for Christian-Muslim Relations', Centre for Islamic

Studies and Christian-Muslim Relations, London School of Theology, April 2010, pp. 4–14.

[11] S. Saggar and J. Drean, *British Public Attitudes and Ethnic Minorities* (London: Cabinet Office, July 2001).

[12] 'Record Number of Muslim MPs Elected in 2019 General Election', 5 Pillars (13 December 2019) https://5pillarsuk.com/2019/12/13/record-number-of-muslim-mps-in-2019-general-election (accessed 7 Sept. 2020).

[13] E. Kaufmann, 'Europe's Muslim Future', *Prospect* (April 2010).

[14] 'Europe's Growing Population', Pew Research Center – Religion and Public Life (29 November 2017) https://www.pewforum.org/2017/11/29/europes-growing-muslim-population (accessed 29 June 2020).

[15] P. Jenkins, *God's Continent: Christianity, Islam, and Europe's Religious Crisis* (New York: Oxford University Press, 2007), pp. 118–19.

[16] Chatham House, *What Do Europeans Think about Muslim Immigrants?* (February 2017). This study found that the percentages of the population who were against any further immigration were 53% in Germany, 63% in Austria, 51% in Italy and 47% in the UK.

[17] A. Taheri, 'What Do Muslims Think?', *The American Interest* 2.5, May/June 2007, p. 12.

[18] Jesus was consistently gracious with Samaritans; see Luke 9:51–56; 10:25–37; 17:11–19; John 4:1–42; 8:2–11, 48; Acts 1:6.

[19] Dr Jenny Taylor, in a summary of the migration process over the past century: 'Immigrant Religious Activism, Government Policies and the Interfaith Challenge', a paper given at a day conference, 'The Numbers Game: Britain's Changing Demographics and the Implication for Christian-Muslim Relations', Centre for Islamic Studies and Christian-Muslim Relations, London School of Theology, April 2010, pp. 15–23.

[20] T. Whitehead, 'Labour Wanted Mass Immigration to Make UK More Multicultural, Says Former Adviser', *The Telegraph* (23 October 2009) https://www.telegraph.co.uk/news/uknews/law-and-order/6418456/Labour-wanted-mass-immigration-to-make-UK-more-multicultural-says-former-adviser.html (accessed 7 Sept. 2020).

[21] The Bradford Commission Report: *The Report of an Inquiry into the Wider Implications of Public Disorders in Bradford*, 9–11 June 1995 (published 1 November 1996).

[22] J. Muhammad Buaben, 'The Numbers Game: A Muslim Perspective on Immigration and Integration', a paper given at a day conference, 'The Numbers Game: Britain's Changing Demographics and the Implication

for Christian-Muslim Relations', Centre for Islamic Studies and Christian-Muslim Relations, London School of Theology, April 2010, p. 29.

23 Turkey's involvement with European integration project began in 1959 at the Ankara Association Agreement (1963). Turkey applied to join the EU in 1987 and became eligible to join it in 1997.

24 The term 'Eurabia' can be traced to a single author, the Egyptian-born Jewish intellectual, Gisèle Littman, who published the book *Eurabia: The Euro-Arab Axis* in 2005 under the name Bat Ye'or.

25 I. Cunningham, 'Asylum Seekers: Fears vs Facts', *Reader's Digest*, October 2002, p. 105.

26 Jenkins, *God's Continent*, pp. 118–19.

27 J. Austin, 'Terror in Manchester: 3,500 Potential Terrorists & 400 ISIS Fighters Back from Syria in UK', *Express* (23 May 2017) https://www.express.co.uk/news/uk/782647/London-terror-attack-3-500-potential-terrorists-monitored-less (accessed 3 Sept. 2020).

28 L. Dearden, 'UK Home to Up to 25,000 Islamist Extremists Who Could Pose Threat, EU Official Warns', *Independent* (1 September 2017) https://www.independent.co.uk/news/uk/home-news/islamist-extremists-uk-highest-number-europe-25000-terror-threat-eu-official-isis-islam-britain-attacks-a7923966.html (accessed 26 Jan. 2021).

29 Taylor, 'Immigrant Religious Activism', p. 20, citing Ed Hussain, *The Islamist: Why I Joined Radical Islam in Britain, What I Saw and Why I Left* (London: Penguin, 2007).

30 B.A. Musk, *Passionate Believing: Why Do Some Muslims Become Fundamentalists?* (London: Monarch, 2003).

31 People with 'Christian' affiliation get involved in violence. The Oklahoma bomber Timothy McVeigh was raised a practising Catholic; Anders Breivik who massacred teenagers in Norway was confirmed as a Lutheran; in East Africa, The Lord's Resistance Army is 'Christian' yet listed as a terrorist group.

32 The term 'hermeneutics' is from the Greek word *hermēneuō*, meaning 'to translate or interpret a text'; see E.D. Hirsch Jr, *Validity in Interpretation* (New Haven, CT: Yale University Press, 1967).

33 Taheri, 'What Do Muslims Think?', p. 15.

34 Pew Research Center, Spring 2017 Global Attitudes Survey, Question 20.

35 Poll conducted by ICM and featured in the TV documentary *What British Muslims Really Think*, Channel 4, 13 April 2016.

36 Pastor Terry Jones of Gainesville, Florida: K. Connolly, 'German Church Disowns Terry Jones, Qur'an-Burning American Preacher', *The Guardian*

(9 December 2010) https://www.theguardian.com/world/2010/sep/09/cologne-church-quran-burning-preacher (accessed 29 Dec. 2020).

37 Pastor Creighton Lovelace, Danieltown Baptist Church, Forest City, North Carolina: https://en.wikipedia.org/wiki/Creighton_Lovelace (accessed 7 Sept. 2020).

38 Professor T. Modood, 'Islamophobia and Reasonable Criticism: Five Tests', given in a lecture in Birmingham, 2010.

8: Mount Occlusion

1 A. Taheri, 'What Do Muslims Think?', *The American Interest* 2.5, May/June 2007, p. 6.

2 'Barna Group: The State of the Church (2019)', ChurchInfluence.com (15 July 2019) https://churchinfluence.com/barna-group-the-state-of-the-church-2019. See also Paul Maxwell PhD in SelfWire, *Why Young Men Are Leaving Evangelicalism*, video, YouTube (13 September 2018) https://youtu.be/EaFpVyYVQ8U (accessed 21 Dec. 2020).

3 Maajid Nawaz, speaking at the annual conference of the National Secular Society, London, 3 September 2016. In Andalucia, Spain, a version of sharia law (i.e. of the Malaki theological school) was imposed as a last resort in order to resist a French military incursion from the north; the other occasion was when the Ottomans, impressed with the adoption of a single system of law in Europe, imposed the version of sharia of the Hanifi theological school.

4 M. Siddiqui, *My Way: A Muslim Woman's Journey* (London: I.B. Tauris, 2015).

5 https://policyexchange.org.uk/wp-content/uploads/2016/09/living-apart-together-jan-07.pdf (accessed 21 Feb. 2021).

6 Taheri, 'What Do Muslims Think?', pp. 16–17.

7 A hadith by Tirmidhi, no. 2641 et al., and as reported by Tabarani in Al-Awsat, no. 7840. Authenticated by a body of Islamic scholars, past and present.

8 A. Shalakany, 'Redefinition of Shari'a Law in Modern Egyptian Legal Thought from 1798 to the Present', *American University in Cairo Today*, Fall 2008, pp. 26–7.

9 R. Pigott, 'Turkey in Radical Revision of Islamic Texts', BBC News (26 February 2008) http://news.bbc.co.uk/1/hi/world/europe/7264903.stm (accessed 25 June 2020).

10 Sheikh Dr Yasir Qadhi, on his YouTube Channel, https://www.youtube. com/user/YasirQadhi/videos (accessed 4 Feb. 2021).

11 'Articles in Saudi Press Call to Amend Thousands of Scribal Errors in the Quran, Reexamine Islamic Texts in Light of Modern Perceptions', Memri (18 August 2020) www.memri.org/reports/articles-saudi-press-call-amend-thousands-scribal-errors-quran-reexamine-islamic-texts-light (accessed 7 Sept. 2020).

12 Dr Taj Hargay, 'My Persecution by the Muslim McCarthyites: Islam Has Been Taken Over by a Distorted Faith. We Need a Reformation to Rescue It', *The Times*, 10 April 2009.

13 M. Nawaz, Quilliam Foundation, 'Multiculturalism Is Dead', speaking on LBC Radio, using Home Office statistics.

14 M. Phillips, *Londonistan: How Britain Is Creating a Terror State Within* (London: Gibson Square, 2006).

15 T. Ramadan, *Radical Reform: Islamic Ethics and Liberation* (New York: Oxford University Press, 2008).

16 British Muslims for Secular Democracy, https://www.bmsd.org.uk (accessed 7 Sept. 2020).

17 Muslim Women's Council, https://www.muslimwomenscouncil.org.uk/ media/news/why-i-want-build-women-led-mosque-britain (accessed 7 Sept. 2020).

18 Muslim Women's Network, http://www.mwnuk.co.uk (accessed 7 Sept. 2020); also Register Our Marriage, https://registerourmarriage.org (accessed 7 Sept. 2020).

19 J. Stewart, 'Welcoming the Convert: Christians and Muslims Working Together to Ensure Religious Freedom', *IDEA Magazine*, July/Aug 2015, pp. 24–5.

20 J.M. Broder, 'For Muslim Who Says Violence Destroys Islam, Violent Threats', *The New York Times*, 11 March 2006.

21 'Abda Khan: Solicitor & Author', Asian Women Mean Business (25 February 2019) https://www.asianwomenmeanbusiness.com/abda-khan-solicitor-author (accessed 7 Sept. 2020).

22 I. Manji, *The Trouble with Islam Today: A Muslim's Call for Reform in Her Faith* (New York: St Martin's Press, 2005).

23 A. Hirsi Ali, *Heretic: Why Islam Needs a Reformation Now* (New York: Harper, 2015).

24 A. Abd al-Raziq, *Islam and the Sources of Political Authority* (1925) http://www.oxfordislamicstudies.com/article/opr/t125/e8 (accessed 7 Sept. 2020). For a modern translation of this book, see A. Abdel Razek,

Islam and the Foundations of Political Power (trans. M. Loufti; Agha Khan University / Edinburgh: Edinburgh University Press, 2012).

25 A.W. El-Affendi, *Who Needs an Islamic State?* (Peterborough: Upfront, 2011).

26 A. Gomaa, *Responding from the Tradition: One Hundred Contemporary Fatwas by the Grand Mufti of Egypt* (Louisville, KY: Fons Vitae, 2012).

27 A.A. An-Na'im, *Towards an Islamic Reformation: Civil Liberties, Human Rights and International Law* (New York: Syracuse University Press, 1996).

28 A. Khan, and Maktaba Islamia, ed., *Exposing the Call for Islamic Reformation: The Battle of Hearts and Minds* (Scotts Valley, CA: CreateSpace, 2015).

29 Taheri, 'What Do Muslims Think?', p. 15.

30 'Internet Usage in the Middle East – Statistics and Trends', infographic, GO-Gulf (2 August 2013) https://www.go-gulf.ae/internet-usage-middle-east/ (accessed 7 Sept. 2020).

31 National Counterterrorism Center USA, *2011 Report on Terrorism* (Washington, DC: Office of the Director of National Intelligence, 2012) https://fas.org/irp/threat/nctc2011.pdf (accessed 22 Sept. 2020).

32 J.L. Allen Jr, 'The War on Christians: Dispatches from the Front Lines of Anti-Christian Persecution', *The Spectator*, 5 October 2013.

33 The Christian Institute, https://www.christian.org.uk (accessed 7 Sept. 2020).

34 Open Doors, https://www.opendoorsuk.org (accessed 7 Sept. 2020).

35 Abdullah Sameer, *Rise of Apostasy*, video, YouTube (1 February 2018) https://youtu.be/_-pYPWc26Gk (accessed 1 Aug. 2020).

36 Abdullah Sameer, *Rise of Apostasy*.

37 T. Green, 'Conversion from Islam to Christianity in Britain', in *Between Naivety and Hostility: Uncovering the Best Christian Responses to Islam in Britain* (ed. Steve Bell and Colin Chapman; Milton Keynes: Authentic, 2011), p. 302.

38 Stewart, 'Welcoming the Convert', pp. 24–5.

39 Joel Rosenberg, *Washington Times*, reported by CWR News International, 3 January 2007.

40 Al-Katani is the president of The Companions Lighthouse for the Science of Islamic Law in Libya, which is an institution specializing in graduating imams and Islamic preachers; see 'Six Million Muslims leave Islam Every Year', Virtue Online, https://virtueonline.org/6-million-muslims-leave-islam-every-year (accessed 4 Feb. 2020).

41 R. Gholami, *Secularism and Identity: Non-Islamiosity in the Iranian Diaspora* (Abingdon: Routledge, 2015).

42 Giordano-Bruno-Stiftung, *10 Years of Ex-Muslims: The Story of an International Human Rights Movement*, video, YouTube (21 July 2018) https://youtu.be/Uu4hDEPYZzs (accessed 16 May 2020).

43 M. Zaidi, *A Dutiful Boy: A Memoir of a Gay Muslim's Journey to Acceptance* (London: Square Peg/Vintage, 2020).

44 British Muslims for Secular Democracy, https://www.bmsd.org.uk.

45 D. Garrison, *A Wind in the House of Islam: How God Is Drawing Muslims around the World to Faith in Jesus Christ* (Monument, CO: WIGTake Resources, 2014), p. 5.

46 D. Garrison, 'The Greatest Turning in History', *IDEA Magazine*, July/Aug 2015, https://www.eauk.org/news-and-views/the-greatest-turning-in-history (accessed 15 March 2021).

47 J. Trousdale, *Miraculous Movements: How Hundreds of Thousands of Muslims Are Falling in Love with Jesus* (Nashville: Thomas Nelson, 2012), pp. 127–40.

48 S. Bell, *Gospel for Muslims: Learning to Read the Bible through Eastern Eyes* (Milton Keynes: Authentic, 2012), pp. 59–65.

9: Mount Mission

1 Donald Rumsfeld, former US Secretary of Defense, in a news briefing on 12 February 2002.

2 J. Stott, *The Lausanne Covenant: An Exposition and Commentary*, Lausanne Occasional Papers 3 (Wheaton IL: Lausanne Committee for World Evangelization, 1975), p. 14, https://www.lausanne.org.

3 Scriptural Reasoning Society, http://www.scripturalreasoning.org.uk; see also the Cambridge Inter-Faith Programme, www.interfaith.cam.ac.uk (accessed 24 June 2020).

4 B.A. Musk, *Kissing Cousins? Christians and Muslims Face to Face* (Oxford: Monarch, 2005), p. 33.

5 C. Moucarry, *Faith to Faith: Christianity and Islam in Dialogue* (Leicester: IVP, 2001), p. 253.

6 Moucarry, *Faith to Faith*, p. 17.

7 R. Newman, *Questioning Evangelism: Engaging People's Hearts the Way Jesus Did* (Grand Rapids, MI: Zondervan, 2000).

8 Rabbi Isser Z. Weisberg, *Between Jews and Christians*, video, YouTube (25 December 2020) https://youtu.be/2A3LLWeacO8 (accessed 28 Dec. 2020).

9 D. Garrison, *A Wind in the House of Islam: How God Is Drawing Muslims around the World to Faith in Jesus Christ* (Monument, CO: WIGTake Resources, 2014), pp. 205–24.

10 B.A. Musk, *The Certainty Trap: Can Christians and Muslims Afford the Luxury of Fundamentalism?* (Pasadena, CA: William Carey Library, 2008).

11 Naga Seminarian, *Ravi Zacharias on Ahmed Deedat*, video, YouTube (26 August 2020) https://www.youtube.com/watch?v=p9lDEmCqZSk (accessed 28 Jan. 2021).

12 J. Hubers, 'Samuel Zwemer and the Challenge of Islam: From Polemic to a Hint of Dialogue', *International Bulletin of Mission Research* 28.3 (July 2004): pp. 117–21.

13 Author anonymous, 'History Reveals Questions about This Approach', Missio Nexus (1 January 1998) https://missionexus.org/history-reveals-questions-about-this-approach (accessed 3 Feb. 2020). The article was posted in response to the article by Jay Smith, 'Courage in Our Convictions: The Case for Debate in Islamic Outreach', *Evangelical Missions Quarterly* 34.1 (January 1998): pp. 28–35.

14 'St. John of Damascus's Critique of Islam', Orthodox Christian Information Center (26 March 2006) http://www.orthodoxinfo.com/general/stjohn_islam.aspx (accessed 29 June 2020).

15 Dr Jay Smith, training objectives for an international webinar course on apologetics/polemics.

16 'Speak Up: Building Confidence in Our Gospel Freedoms', Evangelical Alliance https://www.eauk.org/what-we-do/initiatives/speak-up (accessed 7 Sept. 2020).

10: Grace Pass

1 Naga Seminarian, *Jordan Peterson Dreams about Jesus Christ*, video, YouTube (22 December 2020) https://youtu.be/fcudKSvH058 (accessed 29 Dec. 2020).

2 L. Pachuau, 'Engaging the "Other" in a Pluralist World: Toward a Subaltern Hermeneutics of Christian Mission', *Studies in World Christianity* 8.1 (April 2002): p. 77.

3   A. Walls, *The Cross-Cultural Process in Christian History* (Edinburgh: T&T Clark, 2002), p. 220.

4   See Mark 12:30–32; Rom. 13:8,10; 1 John 3:18; 1 Cor. 13:4–13.

5   See Matt. 28:19–20; Mark 16:15; Luke 24:47; John 20:21; Acts 1:7–8.

6   See Matt. 5:3–10; Rom. 12:18; Phil. 4:9; Jas 3:17–18.

7   John Stott, *The Lausanne Covenant: An Exposition and Commentary*, Lausanne Occasional Papers 3 (Wheaton IL: Lausanne Committee for World Evangelization, 1975), p. 13.

8   Canon J. John at Operation World Conference, The Bridge Community Church, Leeds, September 2019.

9   R. Sudworth, *Distinctively Welcoming: Christian Presence in a Multi-Faith Society* (Milton Keynes: Scripture Union, 2007).

10 Dr J. Taylor, 'Immigrant Religious Activism, Government Policies and the Interfaith Challenge', a paper given at day conference, 'The Numbers Game: Britain's Changing Demographics and the Implication for Christian-Muslim Relations', Centre for Islamic Studies and Christian-Muslim Relations, London School of Theology, April 2010, p. 22.

11 T.S. Eliot, 'Little Gidding', *The Four Quartets* (London: Faber & Faber, 2001).

Further Information

Further information is available on:

- Statistics on attitudes and identities in Britain, at: https://demos.co.uk/press-release/demos-launches-research-hub-on-ethnic-attitudes-and-identities-in-britain (accessed 29 Dec. 2020)
- Ethical guidelines for Christian and Muslim witness in Britain, issued by the Christian Muslim Forum, 2009, at: http://46.101.6.182/wp-content/uploads/2018/12/CMF-Ethical-Guidelines-for-Christian-and-Muslim-Witness-in-Britain.pdf
- Responding to Muslims with 'grace and truth': position statement of the Mahabba Network, at: https://www.mahabbanetwork.com/core-ethos

Gospel for Muslims

*Learning to read the Bible
through eastern eyes*

Steve Bell

While acknowledging the challenging social and political issues
posed by Islam, Steve Bell explains how Muslims access
the gospel more easily when it is identified with the person of
Jesus and his activity on the earth throughout the Bible.

Gospel for Muslims affirms Christ as the 'third way' between Islam
and institutionalized Christianity; and the right of every Muslim
to hear the gospel, change allegiance to Christ and follow Jesus in
culturally appropriate ways.

978-1-85078-880-5

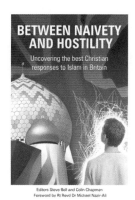

Between Naivety and Hostility

Uncovering the best Christian responses to Islam in Britain

Steve Bell

Enables readers to engage with the issues and come to conclusions that might help them be better social peacemakers and spiritual friends to Muslims for the sake of Jesus Christ.

978-1-85078-957-4

Grace for Muslims?

The journey from fear to faith

Steve Bell

Is it possible for Christians to relate to Muslims without being politically naive or theologically liberal? Steve Bell believes it is. He shares his own journey and reflects upon the process through which he arrived at the crucial ingredient - grace.

978-1-85078-664-1

The Good God

Enjoying Father, Son and Spirit

Michael Reeves

Why is God love? *Because God is a Trinity.*

Why can we be saved? *Because God is a Trinity.*

How are we able to live the Christian life? *Through the Trinity.*

In this lively and refreshing book, we find an accessible introduction to the profound beauty of the Trinity. With wit and clarity, Reeves draws from notable teachers from church history to the present to reveal how the Christian life is rooted in the triune God - Father, Son and Spirit. Be encouraged to grow in enjoyment of God and see how God's triune being makes all his ways beautiful.

978-1-84227-744-7

Christ Our Life

Celebrating the joy of knowing Jesus

Michael Reeves

How can we know who God is? *We look to Jesus.*
How can we live a godly life? *We look to Jesus.*
How do we know we can be saved? *We look to Jesus.*

In this lively and refreshing book, we find an accessible introduction to the profound glory and wonder of Christ. With wit
and clarity, Michael Reeves, author of bestselling *The Good God*,
draws from notable teachers from church history to the present to
reveal a deeper and richer understanding of who Jesus is, his life
on earth, his death and resurrection and his anticipated return.
Rather than just merely adding to our knowledge about Jesus, this
book is a call to consider Christ more deeply so that he might
become more central for you, that you might know him better,
treasure him more, and enter into his joy.

Be encouraged to look upon Jesus and see how he is indeed our
life, our righteousness, our holiness and our hope.

978-1-84227-758-4

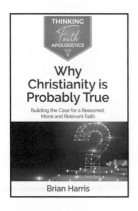

Why Christianity is Probably True

*Building the case for a reasoned,
moral and relevant faith*

Brian Harris

Does the Christian faith lack intellectual, moral and experiential credibility?

These are the three most common accusations made against the Christian faith today. Brian Harris examines each of these arguments in turn by outlining the issue, looking at evidence against the claim before evaluating the argument as a whole.

This book explores these questions in a rigorous but accessible way. It doesn't offer easy, solve-everything answers, but it does build a cumulative case based on reason, history and experience to suggest that God probably exists, and that the Christian understanding of God could well be valid.

978-1-78893-106-9

The Goldsworthy Trilogy

Three classic books in one volume

Graeme Goldsworthy

This book represents excellent value, combining three Goldsworthy classics in one volume: *Gospel and Kingdom*, *Gospel and Wisdom*, and *Gospel in Revelation*.

Combined, these books provide an excellent model for understanding the Christian interpretation of Scripture in both the Old and New Testaments. *Gospel and Kingdom* is concerned with finding the gospel principles inherent in the Pentateuch and historical books of the Old Testament; *Gospel and Wisdom* applies the same objective with regard to the Wisdom literature of Proverbs, Ecclesiastes, and Job. *Gospel in Revelation* demystifies the notoriously difficult Apocalypse by reference to the gospel theme uniting the startling visions.

978-1-84227-036-3

Mission in Marginal Places

The Stories

Paul Cloke & Mike Pears (Eds)

The *Mission in Marginal Places* series aims to provoke new understandings about how to respond to a very basic question: how might Christians respond to the Spirit's invitation to participate in God's love for the world, and especially in places of suffering and healing, of reconciliation and justice?

The third book, *The Stories*, is an exploration of the processes and practices of 'storying' mission; of listening to others and then telling appropriate stories about interconnected lives.

978-1-78078-185-3

Mission in Marginal Places: The Theory
978-1-84227-9

Mission in Marginal Places: The Praxis
978-1-84227-910-6

Our Precious Lives

*Why telling and hearing stories
can save the church*

Steve Morris

In a world of increasing social fragmentation and loneliness,
Our Precious Lives demonstrates how listening to others can be
transformational in creating a sense of belonging. Inspiring stories
are grounded by practical ideas to put storytelling at the heart
of the church, and questions in each chapter encourage us all to
glimpse more of God, revel in our uniqueness and realize that we
all have something valuable to offer as his followers.

Underpinned by practical pastoral experience, this is a book full
of quirky and unexpected life stories that open us up afresh to the
beauty of life and our God.

978-1-78893-079-6

The Divine Spark

*Why Celtic wisdom can refresh
the church today*

Steve Morris

Can the ancient model of Celtic Christianity really have any
relevance to our charismatic, evangelical churches?

Celtic Christianity was always on the margins of society, so
looking at how those Christians lived out their faith can bring
real insight into how we model church today. From slowing down
in a busy world, reconnecting with God through appreciating
nature, caring for the planet, to finding God's presence through
mindfulness and practising whole-life discipleship, there are
treasures to be found that are surprisingly modern and relevant to
the world we live in today.

Discover how the Celtic tradition can revitalise and reconnect us
in our daily walk with God.

978-1-78893-177-9

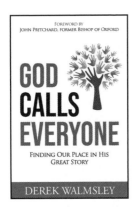

God Calls Everyone

*Finding our place in
his great story*

Derek Walmsley

What are we supposed to do with our lives? Does God have a plan
for us?

If you have ever asked these questions, then this book will help
you to discern what your vocation might be. Through the lens of
the Bible's whole narrative, you are invited to take part in God's
story, and what he is doing, rather than asking what we can do for
God. Questions at the end of each chapter allow you to reflect on
the characteristics and attitudes needed for serving God.

Whether you are considering full-time ministry or wondering
where you fit into God's plan, this is an accessible and engaging
look at the joyous celebration of God calling us all to be part of
his story.

978-1-78893-108-3

Paternoster:
thinking faith

We trust you enjoyed reading this book
from Paternoster. If you want to be informed
of any new titles from this author and other
releases you can sign up to the Paternoster
newsletter by scanning below:

Online:
authenticmedia.co.uk

Follow us: